The
Clarity Principle

The
Clarity Principle

HOW GREAT LEADERS MAKE THE MOST
IMPORTANT DECISION IN BUSINESS
(and What Happens When They Don't)

Chatham Sullivan

A Wiley Brand

Published by Jossey-Bass

A Wiley Brand

One Montgomery Street, Suite 1200, San Francisco, CA 94104-4594—
www.josseybass.com

Jossey-Bass books and products are available through most bookstores. To contact Jossey-Bass directly call our Customer Care Department within the U.S. at 800-956-7739, outside the U.S. at 317-572-3986, or fax 317-572-4002.

Wiley publishes in a variety of print and electronic formats and by print-on-demand. Some material included with standard print versions of this book may not be included in e-books or in print-on-demand. If this book refers to media such as a CD or DVD that is not included in the version you purchased, you may download this material at http://booksupport.wiley.com. For more information about Wiley products, visit www.wiley.com.

Library of Congress Cataloging-in-Publication Data
Sullivan, Chatham, 1976–
  The clarity principle : how great leaders make the most important decision in business (and what happens when they don't) / Chatham Sullivan.—First edition.
     pages cm
  Includes bibliographical references and index.
  ISBN 978-1-118-43466-6 (cloth); ISBN 978-1-118-62727-3 (ebk);
ISBN 978-1-118-63068-6 (ebk); ISBN 978-1-118-63071-6 (ebk)
  1. Leadership. 2. Decision making. I. Title.
  HD57.7.S85 2013
  658.4'092—dc23

                                                2012049785

Printed in the United States of America

FIRST EDITION

HB Printing   10 9 8 7 6 5 4 3 2 1

To my family
Elizabeth, Sophia, Abraham, and Lyra

Contents

The
Clarity Principle

Introduction

Three hundred senior managers of a Fortune 500 consumer goods company sat patiently in a ballroom of a posh San Francisco hotel. Like me, they were there to hear important news. Leadership changes, restructuring, and questions about the company's strategy had spread confusion throughout the organization. The assembled group hoped for some clarity.

As a consultant, my job was to help the group discuss the implications of the new strategy later that day. The company's senior executives had worked right up to the eleventh hour, and I knew only the bare outlines of what they were going to reveal. I was curious myself to see what would happen.

It started well enough. The morning had been finely choreographed. Professional videographers patrolled the perimeter of the room while a succession of senior executives delivered warm-up speeches for the new strategy. Introduced by tasteful selections of contemporary rock hits, the executives passed by the company's supersized logo which adorned a backlit wall above center stage. Like presenters at the Oscars, the executives traded playful banter at the podium. Some offered heartfelt pep talks about the future. Others shared stories. It was scripted, but good-humored. They seemed to know the right words to say. One executive declared, "We have to make big choices."

Good, I thought from my perch in the back of the room. *This sounds pretty serious. They might get something started today.*

Two hours later my optimism had faded. The trailer had been better than the movie. Beyond the 2 × 2 that summarized the strategy, the bullet points, and the management speak, the new strategy didn't say much. If anything, it confused rather than clarified. It was vague, equivocal, and short on substance for people in the room. It certainly didn't satisfy the bigger questions that I knew were on everybody's minds.

Sitting at the back of the ballroom, I looked around to observe the audience reaction. I craned my neck to see the expressions of managers in the row of tables directly in front of me. It wasn't good. I saw hints of exasperation and cynicism. People stirred and shifted in their seats, or shot quick glances at one another. The bolder ones expressed their feelings in harsh whispers ("What's really different?"); the majority held their tongues, nodded, or else sighed in resignation. Then, as the wagon train of speakers rolled on, I imagined that the assembled managers were already beginning to work out in their heads what they would say to their people back home— people who were waiting for answers.

As for me, I sank down in my chair and stared into the vast space above the ballroom. My job didn't hang in the balance. I was just a consultant. Still, I felt a mixture of disappointment and frustration. Not because my task for the afternoon had become more difficult, but because I had seen this movie too many times before. It was one more example of a company that couldn't get clear about what it was.

Identity Crisis

Every company, including yours, exists for a reason. Every business has a purpose. Even if your organization's objective is to make money, the way it endures is by solving a particular kind of problem in the world. Whether you are a pharmaceutical carving out a unique way to treat patients, a nonprofit serving a worthy constituency, or a global retailer satisfying a particular consumer desire, your market, your customers, and the people in your organization all need to know clearly what the business is about. Just like individuals, companies need to know "who" they are, what they're up to, and why it matters.

As the following chapters will show, businesses that clearly understand and express their purpose outperform those that don't. Clarity of purpose, I'll argue, is a competitive imperative. It's also an existential one. Purpose, and the identity it conveys, is the lifeblood of the organization. It's what gives a business its driving motive and cohering storyline.

But purpose doesn't happen by default. *It's chosen.* The viability of the strategy wasn't the real problem in San Francisco that day. It wasn't a matter of formulating the right market position or finding the right words or communicating the right messages. The problem was that when it came time to make the big choice, the company and its leaders blinked. They were unwilling to take a stand on the company's core purpose and make a decision.

Having worked closely with executives in Fortune 100s, owner-led businesses, assorted nonprofits, and cultural institutions, I have found that the majority of these organizations—whether great or small—become confused at times about who and what they are. Like the company in the opening vignette, their leaders feign clarity but cannot articulate what they're truly up to. Through their leaders' decisions and actions, these companies unwittingly, but systemically, avoid answering fundamental questions about the business. Some duck the responsibility. Others pretend they have the answer when they do not. But by whatever means, the problem of purpose remains unaddressed. These organizations persistently project an incoherent image to the world. This is an increasingly common condition in business that I think can appropriately be referred to as an "identity crisis."

For those of you who've heard the term, I use identity crisis in much the same way it was originally used, by the psychologist Erik Erikson, to describe an individual whose personality has not matured coherently enough to know who they are or to determine the course of their own life. Although it may seem unusual to transpose a psychological concept onto business, we'll see that the analogy is powerfully applicable. Your business, just like a person, must lay claim to an identity in the world. Your company has to take a stand on what—or who—it is. When it can't—when the business's identity and purpose become vague to its market, customers, and employees—a crisis ensues.

The Clarity Principle expounds a simple idea. Clarity is derived from purpose, and purpose from a pivotal act of choice that leaders make about the business. The goal of this book is to illuminate how difficult it is to define your business, the costs you incur when you fail to clarify your purpose, and the tremendous gains to be won by succeeding in that effort. I will argue that the act of choosing a purpose is the most fundamental activity in business. As we'll see, the task has all the drama, conflict, and potential for transformation that you would expect from something so important.

The Failure to Choose

Back in 1960, Ted Levitt, a beloved lecturer at the Harvard Business School, posed what endures as the quintessential question in management: "What business are you in?" Levitt's work introduced leaders to a new kind of organizational self-consciousness.[1] He insisted that companies think through who they are and why they exist. Using now-iconic examples, he showed how organizations misconstrue their purposes. "Railroad companies think they are in the business of making trains," Levitt declared, "when really they are in the transportation business." Levitt argued that companies that define their business incorrectly face irrelevancy. Railroads, for example, missed the impact of the automobile because they focused all their energy on making bigger and faster trains rather than on solving the principal job of moving people across the country. Levitt was unequivocal about where to place the blame for defining the business incorrectly. "The failure," he wrote, "is at the top."

But even Levitt might sympathize with today's leaders, including my consumer-goods client in San Francisco.

Although his message is still relevant, it must be applied in radically different conditions.

My colleagues and I often hear from our clients that the scale of change that will occur over the next ten years is likely to surpass that of the last fifty. This may prove to be true, but a more vital fact is that the *kind* of change is changing. To borrow the useful terminology of Clay Christensen (a Harvard Business School professor, Christensen developed the concept of disruptive innovation and is the world's foremost authority on the topic), we can be said to live in a *disruptive* era. Technological and business model innovation has uprooted the foundations of many industries. Music, publishing, and media were only the beginning. Early signs of the sea changes to come can already be seen in sectors as diverse as healthcare, retail, financial services, energy, and consumer goods. It's very possible that the shadow of future disruption has already been cast on your industry—or that you're right in the middle of it.

As an illustration, consider the rate of churn in the Standard & Poor's 500. In the 1960s, the average tenure of a company on the S&P list was sixty years. As of this writing, if your company is listed on the S&P 500 you can expect to remain there a mere fifteen years. In five years that tenure is expected to shrink even more. At this pace only 25 percent of the current S&P will remain on the list by 2027.[2] Think about companies in the news lately. Research in Motion (RIM), the company that brought us the BlackBerry, was once blessed with a huge installed base in corporate America. Their market share eroded almost overnight, plummeting from a high watermark of 55 percent market share to 15 percent in less than two years. As companies quickly fall, others rise. Facebook, a company that didn't even exist eight years ago, was worth $100 billion at the point of its IPO.

Could that have happened twenty years ago? I think not. Companies and their purposes come and go, and they do so quickly and under conditions of greater uncertainty. Although in the past, your business might have had to reinvent itself every ten to fifteen years, you may now need to reevaluate your role and position in the market on much shorter cycles. Many businesses have abandoned traditional strategic planning altogether for a more fluid process of constant adaptation. Like chameleons increasing their odds of survival, they change colors as the environment dictates. If the world is so uncertain, why commit at all?

In a disruptive and highly uncertain world, the problem isn't that companies define themselves incorrectly—that is, that they, like the railroads, make a choice distorted by their history or their assumptions about the market. No, the problem today is that *companies don't choose at all*. Choosing, as we'll see, is a risky prospect, fraught with personal, political, and cultural risks for the organization and its leaders. In some cases the failure to choose is a willful irresolution. Leaders intentionally dodge the big questions about the business. In others, the failure is an implicit looking away or an artful compromise across competing strategic ideas about what the business should be. But beneath it all leaders duck their responsibility for choosing because they cannot accept the tradeoffs, risk, and loss that accompany an act of commitment to one definition of the business over another. In a word, leaders are *conflicted* about what the company should be. This avoidance of choice and its pernicious impact on the vitality of a business, as well as its galvanizing solution, is the focus of this book.

What then is an identity crisis in the business realm? Put simply, it is parade of symptoms that occur in the absence of purpose. It occurs when your organization becomes confused about what it is, torn among competing alternatives of what to be. Do we serve this client or that one? Do we fulfill this mission or another? Do we occupy this position in the market or that one? Do we compete on this capability or that? Are we one firm or several? In the context of shifting markets, quickly aging business models, complex company politics, and conflicting pressures on the business, an increasing number of companies—nonprofits included—struggle to make a clear choice about what business they're in. When this happens, their identity becomes incoherent, and a crisis—which may last for years—settles in.

To illustrate the confusion born of a crisis, here are a few examples taken from press reports:

"The Gap struggles to find an identity in today's crowded shopping mall. And Gap's namesake stores, meanwhile, are stuck in the middle: too pricey to be cheap chic but too cheap to be chic."[3] (*Washington Post*)

"Dell is struggling to find its identity in a world dominated by giants like Oracle, IBM, and even Hewlett-Packard, which offer corporate customers a far larger menu of hardware, software, and service than Dell."[4] (*Fortune*)

"Starbucks seems to be in a period of identity crisis, caught between two cultures, needing to change but unsure of what new path to pursue."[5] (*Chicago Tribune*)

These snippets capture the outward signs of an identity crisis. According to the analysts, Dell, Starbucks, and Gap are trapped between positions in the market in a way that points to a muddled identity. Is Dell a personal computer manufacturer or a business-to-business provider of integrated technology solutions? Can Starbucks be an intimate coffee house when there's one on every corner? Is Gap a purveyor of *cheap chic* or *quality classics*?

Ultimately, as we'll see, identity is about *purpose*. Purpose is your organization's reason for being in the world, what we might call your company's "problem-to-solve." Purpose isn't about a specific product or service, but about the calling your company answers in the market. Apple, for example, is an answer to a problem. In a market full of clunky, undifferentiated mass-market products, Apple offers creative, simple, elegant, and highly integrated consumer electronics and software. I would argue that whether you articulate it or not, your company exists in the context of a problem-to-solve. Helping you understand and solve that problem is the crux of this book.

Choosing is an ongoing activity. All companies—including Apple, including yours—are dynamic, existing always in a process of *becoming* rather than a stable state of *being*. They gain, lose, and reinvent their purpose all the time. But this impermanence doesn't mean that your company—even if it's successful—can afford to stop defining itself. In the contemporary business world, the battle against ambiguity is never ending. Defining the business is essential.

Even a stalwart like Walmart can lose touch with its problem-to-solve. From the beginning, the big box retailer's position was "Always Low Prices." It didn't matter if the unit was a bottle of detergent or a pair of shorts; Walmart's purpose and identity were all about providing rock-bottom prices to people who didn't want (or couldn't afford) to spend more money.

But then Walmart tweaked its purpose. Seduced by the prospect of adding a few points to their margin, they invited customers to "look beyond the basics"—shop for cheap products but also entertain more upscale merchandise, such as 500-thread-count sheets.[6] Walmart thought it could entice customers to make a few higher-cost purchases that would boost store sales. The strategy backfired, and after a period of self-examination, the company reclaimed its purpose, cut prices, and announced a new tagline: "Saving people money so they live better lives." In addition to recalibrating their brand image, the clarification of purpose was operationalized through the company's pricing strategy, supply chain, and merchandising. Walmart's actions show that purpose is not an empty slogan—it touches every corner of the business—and that redefining and sometimes reclaiming that purpose is a critical leadership task.

Still, choice is an act burdened with risk, drama, and angst for a business and its leaders. You can often feel this dynamic in critical conversation at the top. In the middle of a conversation with the CEO and the top thirty leaders of a global marketing firm, I witnessed a vice president of strategy give voice to the inertia and anxiety that can afflict a leader of a business in the throes of an identity crisis. "We are collectively afraid," he said to his colleagues, "of making the wrong strategic decision about the business we are in." And further, "Until we take a stand, we will continue to struggle to unite our teams, drive our business, and achieve great results."

When I asked the group, "What is your particular role in the market? What are you guys really doing?" the executive team came up with vague, unconvincing answers. They couldn't articulate an overarching logic to the business. Moreover, they were distraught over being unable to answer the question clearly. The identity crisis was like the proverbial elephant in the room—something everyone understood viscerally but couldn't confront directly. Yet the heat in the vice president's words and his colleagues' response revealed an emerging awareness that something crucial was missing.

Externally, purpose creates coherence and renders your business intelligible to customers in the market. As we'll see, clarity in the marketplace is critical. But the function of purpose within the organization is even more vital. Competing ideas and inconsistencies about identity can permeate the very fabric of your business. Over time, these clashing threads become woven into patterns of enterprise behavior through incentive systems, reporting structures, the dynamics of the culture, and the relationships among individual employees and groups. Like a pattern that repeats itself at larger and smaller scales, an identity crisis shows up everywhere in the business.

For example, contradictions in the identity of the business are often reflected in its most painful patterns of behavior. Turf wars, dysfunctional teams, conflicts between departments, and instances of poor execution are all signs of a deeper conflict about the purpose of the organization. Indeed, I argue—and will show through examples—that even interpersonal conflicts that we view as isolated "people issues" are often actually instantiations of bigger questions about the business. They are events with a common cause, the widespread symptoms of an identity crisis.

This book will show you that it doesn't have to be this way. Leaders and managers can learn to identify and resolve the crisis, and those suffering from its symptoms can learn to alleviate them. Indeed, the conflict underlying the crisis, once identified and transformed into choices to be made by leaders, can transform an organization. Tensions once avoided become fertile ground for innovation and reinvention—a wellspring of energy, creativity, meaning, and community for the business.

This kind of alchemy won't be easy. As we'll see, the transition from crisis to clarity places a tremendous burden on leadership. There are myriad, compelling reasons leaders often avoid, rather than confront, the underlying anxieties that afflict their organizations and why they evade the momentous decisions that define the business and its future. A clear purpose—that most precious of assets—doesn't come cheap, as the stories in this book will attest. But I will show you that the work of choosing a purpose is worth it. This pivotal act isn't just the crucial antidote to the identity crisis, it is the definitive act that provides the North Star that guides and animates the business.

From Crisis to Clarity

Unfortunately, there's no recipe for finding purpose, and so this book isn't like a cookbook. Instead, it is designed to show, through stories, evidence, and insight, what happens in a company when an identity crisis occurs, why it occurs, and what the solution looks like.

We begin our journey by getting a feel for the crisis itself in Chapter One, "Proxy Wars." There are signs and symptoms of a crisis that allow us to diagnose its outbreak. These symptoms tell us an extraordinary amount about how businesses really work. We'll see, in the rather dramatic tale of Donna Dubinsky, how complex, often painful dysfunctions in organizations are enactments of bigger strategic questions. We'll begin to understand how tensions felt throughout the organization often originate in the executive suite—in this case, between Steve Jobs and Apple CEO John Sculley—only to spill over to do collateral damage elsewhere in the enterprise.

In Chapter Two, "The Murky Middle," we'll discover that the heart of the crisis is an insoluble dilemma. Confusion emerges when a company tries to be two things at once, but neither successfully. Through a number of stories, anchored by the ten-years-in-the-making saga at CNN, we will come to understand how shifts in the market demand fate-making choices about the identity of a company, and how a crisis arises when leaders fail to choose between competing notions of the business. Chapter Two ends with a glimpse of the considerable burden leaders face as they confront the most important decisions about the business.

In Chapter Three, "Neither Fish Nor Fowl," we'll turn our attention outward. The market has no sympathy for companies that don't know what they are. This chapter illustrates the stiff penalty that companies pay in the market for lacking both purpose and a clear identity. We'll examine an array of evidence from the worlds of branding, strategy, and economics, making a case for why companies with strong, clear, and meaningfully differentiated identities tend to outperform their rivals.

This brings us to Chapter Four, "The Shadow Side of Strategy." Most of us view business as a rational enterprise. The foundations of business, we believe, can be properly understood through the analysis of revenues, costs, market share, and other metrics of performance. Executives, according to this worldview, are mostly objective decision-makers. However, we'll see in this chapter that that's not always the case. Looking more closely at the causes of an identity crisis, we see that emotional, political, and often very personal dynamics compel leaders to avoid choosing; moreover, those forces are often far beyond their conscious awareness. In fact, the tangled web of breakdowns, failures to execute, and the inability of the business to make meaningful progress often has its roots not in poor decision making per se, but in the unacknowledged failure to define the business. We'll learn that, rather than being a straightforward problem that can be surfaced and resolved, an identity crisis often *cannot even be discussed*. It is a problem that everyone feels but no one dares to confront.

The concluding chapters focus on solutions. In Chapter Five, "Taking a Stand," I will show how a variety of organizations—both renowned and unsung—have resolved their identity crises. I'll offer behind-the-scenes insights on leaders who brought clarity to their businesses through acts of choice and courage. In the context of an identity crisis, choosing goes beyond the rational calculus of looking at the numbers and evaluating sets of strategic options. In many cases, the choice is existential in nature: in order to resolve the crisis and bring purpose to the organization, leaders must take a stand regarding the business. They must make a defining commitment. Many of the stories in this chapter are drawn from my firsthand experience of what these leaders sacrificed, what they gained, and how they generated meaning that brought clarity to the enterprise—to the benefit of both its people and its position in the marketplace.

Chapter Six, "The Hunger for Purpose," illustrates what an organization gains through purpose. We'll look at the power of shared identity through the organizational lens, demonstrating how purpose gives your organization its motive and life force. Purpose provides an organizing principle and logic that gives order, shape, and reason to your organization's activities. As such, purpose helps managers navigate the complexity of the business and make sound, rational decisions. We'll see how purpose establishes a sense of community and meaning for a company.

Finally, the Epilogue will describe how everyone—executive, manager, and even frontline employee—can begin to address a crisis.

• • •

This book is for everyone. For the strategist: I hope you will find a deeper understanding of the political, communal, and often emotional dimensions of strategic choice. For the employee: you may well see reflected in these stories some of your own complicated experiences in the workplace and learn how to understand them not just as personal events but also as expressions of larger struggles in the business. Leaders, especially executives, are a special audience for this book. The following chapters will demonstrate that you have a profound responsibility for taking a stand on what you believe the business is (and is not), and for making the defining choice about its purpose.

To readers of all types, I would make one request before we begin. Because the issues described in this book are as much viscerally felt as intellectually understood, and you may have been in any number of situations like those I describe—and may have felt their impact—I invite you to read this book actively, to the extent that it is helpful to do so. Search out those ideas and stories that hit closest to home, those situations and characters that resonate, and reflect on how they might give you new insights about your own organization. Most important, consider how you might take action based on those insights. If this book does nothing more than give you a cause for action, it will have accomplished its primary objective.

1

Proxy Wars

In 1985, Apple Computer was riding the early wave of the microcomputer revolution. Cofounder and CEO Steve Jobs was among the leading rebels. But the main character in the story I want to tell is Donna Dubinsky, a talented operations manager who came to serve as a kind of canary in the coal mine of Apple's first leadership crisis. (Though I draw from a variety of Apple and industry sources, I rely extensively on the very well documented 1995 Harvard Business School case, "Donna Dubinsky and Apple Computer, Inc.," written by research associate Mary Gentile under the supervision of Prof. Todd D. Jick.[1] My depiction of Donna Dubinsky's crisis largely retells the story as it was vividly related by Prof. Jick and Ms. Gentile. Unless otherwise indicated, quotes from Dubinsky and others are taken from the HBS case.)

Donna and Apple

Donna Dubinsky's star rose quickly at Apple. Forgoing lucrative positions on Wall Street, the Harvard Business School graduate wanted to be close to customers. For her first gig out of school, Dubinsky landed a job in Apple's customer-support team. It was 1981.

It didn't take her long to make an imprint on the company. Under the tutelage of mentor Roy Weaver, Dubinsky grew into an accomplished manager. She ran a tight ship, cultivated a sense of loyalty among her team, and could hold her own with other leaders when needed. "She says what she thinks," noted one senior manager at the time. "If she's right and she loses her issue, she goes down fighting."

By the beginning of 1985, Dubinsky had already been promoted enough times that she was managing all of sales administration, inventory control, customer relations, and the six field warehouses that provided Apple dealers with Mac and Apple II computers. Distribution was her baby, and at Apple in the mid-1980s, distribution mattered. At that time, retailers couldn't afford to carry their own inventory and depended on the efficiency of Apple's distribution system. Dubinsky's organization fulfilled this role admirably. The group had never caused a delay in product delivery, even with record shipment sizes.

Apple, too, was riding high. A year earlier, in January 1984, the Macintosh (the Mac) had made a grand entrance into the personal computer market with its iconic—and iconoclastic—$1.5 million Super Bowl commercial. Two days after that, at the Apple annual shareholder meeting, Apple cofounder Steve Jobs had put on the first of his now famous product revelations. The story he told was about David versus Goliath, Apple versus IBM, creativity and spirit versus Big Brother. Apple was out to take on the world. Here is how former Apple executive Andy Hertzfeld recalls the dramatics of the Jobs keynote speech:

> The crowd is in a frenzy now, as the already famous 1984 commercial, which was shown for the first and only time during the Super Bowl two days ago, fills the screen, featuring a beautiful young woman athlete storming into a meeting of futuristic skinheads, throwing a sledge-hammer at Big Brother, imploding the screen in a burst of apocalyptic light. By the time the commercial is finished, everyone in the auditorium is standing and cheering. All this time, a lone Macintosh has been sitting in its canvas carrying case near the center of the stage. Steve walks over to the bag and opens it up, unveiling the Mac to the world for the very first time. The Macintosh becomes the first computer to introduce itself, speaking in a tremulous voice:
>
> "Hello, I am Macintosh. It sure is great to get out of that bag!"
>
> Pandemonium reigns as the demo completes. Steve has the biggest smile I've ever seen on his face, obviously holding back tears as he is overwhelmed by the moment. The ovation continues for at least five minutes before he quiets the crowd down.[2]

Dubinsky and Apple were on a run. But by the spring of 1985, just a little over a year after Jobs's speech, the good times came to a dramatic end. Apple reached what many, looking back later, believe was the lowest point in the company's grand history. By June, *InfoWorld*, one of the leading computing magazines at the time, featured a rainbow-colored apple icon torn down the middle, with the header "Can Apple Hold Together?"

Given the popularity of the Mac and Dubinsky's rapid ascendance, you would have faced long odds betting that both would stumble—that Apple would be against the ropes and Dubinsky would be writing her resignation letter—or that both, with the indomitable spirit they shared, would eventually find themselves back on top again. But that is exactly what happened. More than just a corporate melodrama, the story of Donna Dubinsky and Apple Computer that I tell here shows a company in the grip of an identity crisis—and the impact of that crisis on the people in the company.

I often use the Donna Dubinsky story when I teach classes of business executives. Dubinsky's story has a way of seeping into the minds of executives who encounter the case. I have discovered that leaders' reactions to the story often reveal more about their own organizations than about the content of the case itself. To that extent, Dubinsky's story is like the famous Rorschach inkblot personality test, wherein respondents, in describing what a series of ambiguous blots of black and multicolored inks looks like to them, reveal something about their innermost desires, worries, and conflicts. This story works in a similar way for the managers I teach and for the organizations they inhabit.

For that reason, I will tell the Dubinsky story in parallel with another. A number of years ago, I was running a leadership session for a group of senior managers at an influential financial institution (which I'll call BBL to protect its confidentiality). So immersed in the case was the class of executives that I eventually realized they were no longer talking about Dubinsky or Apple Computer; instead, they were talking about themselves. By the end of the session, the group had played out its own compressed version of the Dubinsky story. The parallel between what happened at Apple and the story they told in the room that day was so uncannily illuminating for me that in my mind now the two tales are inseparable. Thus the only proper way for me to tell the Dubinsky story is to pair it with the story of the BBL managers. What the BBL managers came to appreciate is that they, like Donna Dubinsky, had become unwitting participants in the larger strategic conflict in their business.

Better to Be a Pirate

The good cheer that had prevailed at the Mac launch festivities in January 1984 had begun to cool by the following fall. Between 1983 and 1985 Apple's market share in the personal computer segment plummeted from 45 percent to 25 percent. Meanwhile, IBM surged ahead. During the period that Apple was declining, Big Blue's PC business grew from zero to a 30 percent market share. Though operating revenues continued to rise for Apple, net income fell, due in part to the Mac's high market-entry costs. To be sure, the Mac had launched well. Sales were impressive. But the computer hadn't come close to meeting sales projections. More important, the Mac presented a fatal challenge to the company's reigning breadwinner, the Apple II.

From the beginning, the conflict between the Mac and the Apple II had the potential to become a problem of existential proportions. Far from being an incremental improvement over the Apple II, the Mac was designed to be a great leap forward in "user-friendly" computing. As such, it had warranted the revolutionary imagery of the Super Bowl commercial. In time the Mac was likely to expand the consumer market by making computing far more accessible to the rest of us—meaning we, the less-technical masses. The Apple II, by contrast, was used primarily in the educational space and still a product for computing enthusiasts, closer in kind to the early computer "kits" that geeky hobbyists sent away for. Put simply, the two products addressed distinctly different problems-to-solve in the market and thus represented different purposes for the company. It was therefore not lost on those within Apple, in 1984, that the Mac represented a fork in the road for the business, just as it did for the entire industry.

The sibling rivalry between Apple II and Mac began at the Mac's conception. Seeking to free Macintosh designers from the bureaucracy of the larger organization, Steve Jobs split the Mac division off from the rest of the business. Jobs made the move with characteristic bravado. "Better to be a pirate," he quipped, "than join the navy." Members of the new division played their part with gusto. Not long after the breakout, the Mac team hoisted a black skull and crossbones flag over the new Mac building.

In the wake of the Mac insurgence, the Apple II group— still producing the larger share of revenues for the company— began to feel undervalued. The rest of the organization wondered where the company was heading.

To make the new structure work, Jobs wooed PepsiCo president John Sculley to come run Apple. "Do you really want to sell sugar water," Jobs asked Sculley, "or do you want to come with me and change the world?" Sculley accepted the position, freeing Jobs to take the helm of the fledgling Macintosh division while retaining his role as chairman of the company.

Jobs laid out what would prove to be a complex agenda for Sculley. He charged his new president with bringing discipline and profitability to the business without sacrificing entrepreneurial spirit. Sculley responded in good faith by structuring the business around three divisions: Apple II, Macintosh, and a third division, called shared services, to be run by the newly hired Bill Campbell, a former head football coach and advertising exec. Shared services included marketing, sales, and Dubinsky's distribution group. In what looked like a Steve Jobs sandwich, Sculley had the unenviable job of both supervising and reporting to Apple's pirate wunderkind.

The Distribution "Problem"

In the fall of 1984, Dubinsky and Weaver presented a routine business plan for distribution to Apple's executive team, which included Jobs, Sculley, and Campbell. The meeting was a yearly ritual to discuss the budget. No one foresaw any difficulties. But, surprisingly, Jobs criticized the plan and asked Weaver and Dubinsky to justify the cost structure of the existing distribution system.

The spirited challenge startled both Weaver and Dubinsky. Cost had never been singled out as a problem in distribution. And why, they wondered, would a company that placed most of its resources and energy in product development attack a delivery system that had never caused a delay?

Jobs wasn't finished. On the heels of the meeting, he sought out Macintosh's director of manufacturing, Debi Coleman, and asked her to explore what was then a novel inventory methodology called just-in-time (JIT). Inspired by the successes of the Toyota production system, and enabled by new computerized supply chain-management systems, the businesses of the day were just beginning to experiment with JIT strategies. The work of implementing such systems would be complicated and difficult, requiring wholesale process changes within and across all of the players in a supply chain. Nonetheless, Jobs—who had recently learned from FedEx CEO Fred Smith that IBM had already launched a promising JIT initiative—didn't want Apple to be left behind.

For her part, Dubinsky dismissed the JIT strategy. She suspected that Coleman and the Macintosh manufacturing department she directed might have hidden agendas. Perhaps, Dubinsky thought, Jobs saw the project as a way to distract the company from the Mac's sagging sales.

But it wasn't just hidden motives that made Dubinsky skeptical. Retailers depended on Apple's current distribution system. Dubinsky believed JIT didn't fit their needs; retailers just weren't ready to make the necessary changes. She was thus all the more confused when she heard that Sculley and the executive team actually liked the JIT concept.

The debate now in play, Campbell asked Weaver and Dubinsky to present a review of the current system and make recommendations for improvement. He gave the pair a deadline of mid-December 1984. Meanwhile, Dubinsky heard troubling rumors. Coleman was preparing a proposal to overhaul the distribution model completely (without talking to distribution).

In light of all these maneuverings, Weaver grew uneasy. Before the reorganization, he had reported directly to Sculley. Campbell's takeover of shared services earlier in the year had deprived Weaver of access to Sculley and shaken the relationship between the two men. Weaver also had considerable pride in distribution and felt threatened by Coleman's proposals. Nor was he able to hide the complex feelings behind his position. When Weaver objected to the JIT concept, many felt that he was being defensive. The JIT question was becoming personal.

With Christmas, and the deadline, steadily approaching, distribution activities accelerated to accommodate increased stress on the system. Dubinsky discovered that she couldn't find the personnel or the time to finish the review by mid-December. She requested and was granted an extension, much to her relief.

Just three weeks later, it wouldn't matter. The conflict over distribution would escalate to dangerous proportions.

Breakdown

On a Monday evening in early January, Dubinsky received a call from Weaver. It was the first time he had ever called her at home, and he sounded panicky. Dubinsky was instantly nervous. Weaver said he had learned that Coleman was scheduled to present her distribution proposal on Wednesday at the annual executive meeting.

The news stunned Dubinsky. The meeting was normally for Apple's most senior executive team. Why was Coleman there? Distribution was Dubinsky's area. Why wasn't *she* involved? Weaver directed Dubinsky to put aside all other work and to draft a counterproposal. Dubinsky worked feverishly and, in a single day, created a presentation for Weaver to deliver at the meeting.

The dueling presentations by Coleman and Weaver provoked a contentious and emotional discussion. Jay Elliot, vice president for human resources, rebuked the leaders present, observing that senior management had maneuvered around its middle managers. Why, Elliot asked, was Coleman presenting to Sculley instead of to Weaver, and why wasn't Dubinsky involved? Against a backdrop of growing animosity between a previously close Jobs and Sculley, the senior team took Elliot's comments seriously. They agreed to assign a new task force to address the distribution problem and report back to Campbell. Furthermore, as an expression of commitment to the Apple team, they agreed to accept the task force's recommendations, whatever they might be. They assigned Coleman, Dubinsky, Weaver, and a number of other stakeholders to the team.

Many at the meeting applauded the resolution. But Campbell had been embarrassed by Weaver and Dubinsky's presentation. He saw the task force as a way to get closure without eliciting any more drama. Weaver saw the task force as a second chance. Dubinsky was angry:

"I didn't know why there should be a task force at all. Distribution's our job. . . . I couldn't get out of this mentality that what we had was working so well. The thing had never broken down. Now I was supposed to go back and do this strategy, and I couldn't figure out what problem I was solving."

As could have been expected, the task force quickly stalled. Coleman stressed the cost savings in her proposal; Dubinsky pointed out flaws in Coleman's assumptions and reframed the costing problems, such as they were, around forecasting. Coleman made suggestions; Dubinsky shot them down.

At the same time, the distribution issue had gained wider visibility. It was seen as an opportunity for senior executives to demonstrate their faith in middle management and empower them to make operating decisions. The problem was that middle management could not agree on the right decisions, and things were getting messy. Sculley wanted Jobs off his back. Campbell was frustrated. Weaver was anxious. And Dubinsky, who still couldn't get over the fact that the issue had been snatched away from her in the first place, began to consider jobs at other companies.

Prior to taking the presentation to the executive team, Campbell met once more with the task force to make sure the team was ready to go. He asked, "So you all agree this is what we should work toward?"

Dubinsky sat silently, holding back until the end. When everyone looked her way, even in the face of the pressure to surrender her position, Dubinsky couldn't help but oppose. "No," she said.

Incensed, Campbell abruptly ended the meeting.

"It was like a dripping faucet," observed Dubinsky. "There was all this pressure to agree. So you found a ground to agree on . . . But you know what? I never really believed it."

The Confrontation

April 17, 1985, brought one more dramatic scene. Still churning from the task force meetings, Dubinsky joined forty other senior middle managers at beautiful Pajaro Dunes, California, for a three-day "leadership experience" retreat. Despite the tranquil setting, Dubinsky loathed the very idea of the retreat. Disillusioned by recent experiences in the company, she found little to be positive about.

But as the retreat got started, Dubinsky was pleasantly surprised to discover that she wasn't alone. Here and there people uttered concerns about the organization. Many voiced their frustrations. She began to realize that her colleagues were as confused as she was about the direction of the company.

During one exercise, participants were asked to draw pictures that illustrated the current state of the business. One participant sketched a single boat being steered by two men, one of them controlled by the other. Someone else drew a caricature of Jobs with two hats: one as division chief and the other as chairman of the board. Another picture portrayed the Apple II Division as a lone windsurfer, bobbing on the ocean, wondering which way the wind might blow.

Late on the second day, Sculley rose to address the group. Speaking of Apple's goals and the need for team effort, he likened the enterprise mission to the work of building a grand cathedral. Dubinsky sat quietly but started to seethe. At the height of Sculley's speech, she could no longer suppress her anger. She raised her hand and, when called on, initiated a public showdown with Apple's chief executive. She pointed out contradictions in Sculley's speech and charged that no one could build a cathedral of the kind Sculley described when they lacked the direction to do so. Implicit in Dubinsky's comments were feelings many had but were reluctant to articulate: that it wasn't Sculley, but Jobs who was calling the shots, and that the relationship between the two top leaders had produced confusing messages about Apple's vision for the future. Sculley volleyed back, pointing out to Dubinsky that it was *her* job to make decisions; that the executive team couldn't hand out all the answers on a silver platter. Before they could continue, time ran out and the session ended.

Minutes later, Dubinsky felt the full impact of the confrontation. Colleagues inconspicuously slipped by to commend her bravery, but Dubinsky was troubled. She had stepped into uncharted and surely dangerous waters. It was, as she later recalled, as if she were "alone on the boat as it pulled out, as my friends and colleagues waved from the shore."

That afternoon Dubinsky ran into the Apple II division's senior executive, Del Yocam. Dubinsky respected Yocam and thought he might be able to provide some necessary perspective on the distribution problem. She and Weaver were just too close to it. Dubinsky asked Yocam his opinion of the JIT problem. Yocam responded that he wasn't in a position to evaluate one strategy over another. It might work; it might not. But on one point he was very clear: Yocam held Dubinsky responsible for figuring it out. If she really thought the strategy could help Apple, she should support it; and if she believed it was wrong for the business, then she should stop it. It was that simple.

The straightforwardness of Yocam's advice startled Dubinsky. He held her accountable for *doing the right thing*.

Six years earlier, one of Dubinsky's business school professors had told her that the first thing to do upon graduation
was to pull together her "go-to-hell money." Dubinsky had
taken that advice. At seven o'clock on the morning after the
retreat, she made an urgent call to Campbell, requesting a
meeting. She hung up the phone and took a deep breath. She
was about to bet her career at Apple on one big move.

At the appointed time, Dubinsky met with Campbell. For
two hours they engaged in fierce debate. Dubinsky started by
acknowledging that she hadn't handled herself well. "But," she
said, "distribution is my area, and I will evaluate it myself,
without the interference of an outside task force."

Dubinsky demanded that her autonomy and accountability
be restored. Back and forth she and Campbell went, until there
was simply no place left to go. She delivered an ultimatum.
She said that if Campbell wouldn't consent to her terms, she
would be forced to leave Apple. This time, it was Campbell's
turn to be stunned. Reluctantly, he agreed to speak with Sculley
and to come back the following Monday with an answer.

That weekend Dubinsky drafted a letter of resignation.
Monday morning she called Weaver to tell him about the
conversation. She then waited patiently for Campbell's call.

Proxy War

When I told Dubinsky's story to the BBL managers, I gave
them an opportunity to engage in some small group discussion
together. I asked them what they thought of the distribution
problem and Dubinsky's handling of it. Their reaction was, at

the start, unequivocally harsh. "Dubinsky," they argued, "failed to read the political winds." Instead of adapting and opening up to change, they pointed out, she had closed down. One person noted, "It's like she dug in her heels and refused to acknowledge the change that was taking place around her."

These observations seemed justified. There is a kind of righteousness to Dubinsky that one can easily interpret as rigidity in the face of a threat. Her oppositional stance is, as a number of the managers suggested, likely the shadow side of her steadfast fighting spirit. What in one circumstance had been a source of strength was, in another, a dangerous weakness.

In the group's analysis, if only Dubinsky had been more finely attuned to the machinations around her, she could have crafted a more deft strategy for herself. For example, why not join Coleman and Jobs instead of opposing them? Surely Jobs was right. Isn't it more fun (and career enhancing) to be a pirate than to join the navy? Dubinsky must have seen Macintosh gaining power. But instead of engaging in productive discussion about the future, she dug in and let her personal frustrations take over.

The BBL class then began to come to a consensus. In the leadership lingo of today, they accused Dubinsky of having "derailed." She was guilty, they said, of letting her personal needs get in the way of inevitable change. (It's worth noting that contemporary readers of the case have the benefit of hindsight: they know that JIT methodologies have stood the test of time—no pun intended. But in 1984 they were *not* a no-brainer. Were they worth investigating? Absolutely. Were they obviously appropriate in all cases? Not necessarily.)

Then, just as the BBL group rendered what seemed to be its final verdict, the winds of consensus suddenly shifted. An alternative explanation of the case began to emerge. It started slowly, when a woman in the group drew her classmates' attention to the fact that Dubinsky's colleagues had also been unhappy at Pajaro Dunes. "How do we deal with that fact?" she asked. "Is there more to the story?"

I posed a follow-up question: "What might be happening at Apple that made the distribution issue so loaded?" As the group responded, the conversation accelerated. Someone said that the bigger problem hanging over distribution was the conflict between Apple II and Mac. It hadn't been resolved. Another person noticed that the clash between Dubinsky and Coleman looked an awful lot like the escalating tension between Sculley and Jobs. Then someone else observed how odd it was that Coleman and not Dubinsky had been asked to explore the JIT strategy. It *was* a bit absurd to have someone from manufacturing reinventing distribution without working with distribution.

Finally, a BBL compliance officer offered this pivotal observation. But his comment wasn't just about Apple; it was also about BBL: "We have these dynamics in *our* organization," he said. "It's a proxy war."

Eyebrows rose. People sat up straight. (Such are often the telltale signs that something important has been said.) Asked to explain the term "proxy war," the manager restated what his colleague had suggested: that the conflict between Coleman and Dubinsky was a stand-in for the unresolved contest between Jobs and Sculley. But, he added, the mutual hostility between the two executives was more strategic than personal (indeed, they had previously been friends); their deteriorating relationship mirrored a far bigger tension about the future of the business. On what would Apple pin its future hopes—the Apple II or the Macintosh? How would they kill off one for the other? "The distribution problem," the compliance officer concluded, "is a proxy for bigger problems. I think *we* do this all the time. We act out the stuff that hasn't been worked out about the business. Maybe it's the same thing with Apple."

Whether because their colleague had exposed a sensitive issue at BBL or because he had "cracked" the Apple case, the group began to stir with new energy. Flipping back a few slides to Apple's organizational chart, I asked, "If this is a strategic issue, then why can't Sculley resolve it?"

The group stared at the chart for a few seconds before shouting out answers. The gist of their explanation went something like this: Sculley was caught between two roles: as the CEO, Sculley had to exercise influence over Jobs even as, in a very twisted way, Sculley also reported to Jobs. Not only was Jobs the company's chairman and therefore Sculley's boss, but he also ran the Mac division, which was an internal competitor of the Apple II group. Sculley was effectively checkmated in carrying out his responsibility to settle the bigger strategic dilemma. Because the problem wouldn't go away, the unresolved tensions spilled out, channeling through smaller tributaries like the distribution issue.[3]

At this point, the lesson hit home for the BBL managers: The distribution conflict is a microcosm of bigger things—not just fights in the executive suite between Jobs and Sculley, but larger issues about Apple's strategic identity in the PC market.

It didn't stop there. The class's fresh insights suggest an alternate interpretation of the moment of confrontation at Pajaro Dunes. Along with her colleagues, Dubinsky knew—though perhaps only vaguely—that Jobs and Sculley were not aligned. The frustrations in the room were really about the strategy problem and the conflict at the top, which Sculley needed to address. When Sculley alluded to the building of a "grand cathedral," the dissonance between his lofty metaphor and the feelings in the room must have been intolerable for Dubinsky. She seems to have spoken both out of her own frustration *and* for the other managers in the room.

This interpretation leads us to an interesting question: Might Dubinsky's confrontation with Sculley be better understood not as her acting out her personal frustrations but as her courageously speaking truth to power on behalf of the organization? Their exchange wasn't just about Sculley and Dubinsky as individuals; rather, it expressed, however obliquely, a fundamental question about whose job it is to manage the bigger tensions of the organization.

This line of thinking points to a very different interpretation of the exchange: By asking Sculley for clarity, Dubinsky attempted to return decision making—and hence the conflict—to its source of origin at the top of the business. When Sculley refused, arguing that the onus for working things out lay with Dubinsky and her colleagues ("I can't hand you everything on a silver platter"), it may have been because Sculley himself didn't have the power to assume that kind of leadership. By pushing the issue back to Dubinsky, Sculley in effect conceded his lack of authority to address the bigger questions swirling at the top of the business. The Dubinsky drama was therefore enacting dynamics far beyond Dubinsky herself.

I would suggest that all organizations have these moments, and that they are exceedingly common if one has the eyes to see it. The poet William Blake once said that we can see the whole world in a grain of sand. I think a similar principle holds for organizations. There are critical moments—such as the fight between Dubinsky and Coleman over distribution or the clash between Sculley and Dubinsky at Pajaro Dunes— that instantiate the struggles of an entire company. These moments are microcosms. They give us an entry point to understanding something much deeper about a company and its troubles. In the first case we have a proxy war for the battle between the Apple II and the Mac; in the second, a fight over who has to deal with it. As we'll see, these enactments aren't just a replaying of deeper conflicts in the business; they are also opening points in which change can occur.

Déjà Vu

After lunch, the CEO of BBL joined his senior managers in our class, and I invited the group to share with him some of their insights from the morning. The group began by identifying a number of the company's own challenges, as reflected in the Apple case. As luck would have it, the CEO asked the group whether it had learned how to handle these challenges. "How do you work out issues across parts of our organization," he asked the group, "without escalating every issue to the top team?" It was at this point that a heated exchange took place:

MANAGER 1: John, with all due respect, I don't think you or the top team are giving us clarity. How do we make these decisions when we don't know what has the higher priority?

CEO: You've got to figure it out for yourself. You can't escalate everything. You're leaders. That's why you're here.

MANAGER 2: We could figure it out if we knew what was important and what wasn't. But we don't have a framework for making these decisions. It feels like our being asked to work it out is a setup.

(At this point I could feel the anxiety in the room and decided to push John, the CEO, just a bit further.)

ME: I want to point out a dilemma. John is saying that he and the top team can't field every concern. At the same time, John, the senior managers don't feel confident hashing out differences between departments without a deeper understanding of the strategy, and I think they're saying they need more clarity from you so that the conflicts below don't end up personal. Otherwise it turns into a political football between groups.

(A short, pregnant pause in the conversation)

CEO: You guys should know that we don't have everything worked out yet. What if we told you what we do know and also what we haven't yet figured out? Would that help?

GROUP: Yes! *(Heads nodding)*

The parallel here is striking. In BBL, we have a group of senior leaders who, like Dubinsky and Coleman, have to work out decisions across complex organizational boundaries and get buy-in from individuals over whom they have little formal authority. Fights arise, things get messy, and it's not clear how to adjudicate the issues. The managers ask for a set of strategic priorities to help them evaluate and make decisions in these situations. They need a feeling for what matters given the aims of the business in order to manage their own relationships.

Here in the class, however, the outcome was very different from the one at Pajaro Dunes. The BBL CEO recognized that his own conduct was creating the very behaviors he so adamantly opposed. Though it was clear he lacked a strong point of view on the company's strategic direction, he acknowledged not knowing. The senior managers appreciated that the CEO didn't have everything worked out. Moreover, they didn't (and shouldn't) expect him to—he is human, after all. From this moment of truth emerged a quick negotiation, a proposal to act differently, and an agreement.

Whereas the confrontation with Dubinsky and Sculley ended in an impasse, the one between the BBL CEO and his senior managers concluded with a small, albeit meaningful transformation.

Leaders and managers, take note. Propitious moments like these, which play out larger problems in the business, happen quite often. When they do, you can either be an unwitting participant in the drama, playing out a script of which you have no authorship, or you actively engage the underlying issue. Indeed, as this example suggests, these moments are highly leveragable; they work like small openings through which bigger unresolved issues can be addressed.

One of my goals over the course of this book is to persuade you that much of the dysfunctional, painful, and, as we'll see, often absurd, events in organizations are rooted in bigger tensions within the business. Moreover, if you learn to read these moments for what they are, there are gains to be had. There's a warning here too. It is all too easy to mistake these moments for something less than what they really are. One could have easily tossed off Dubinsky's confrontation with Sculley as an example of a personal derailment or tussle between Dubinsky and Sculley. Indeed, that kind of interpretation is the norm for most of us. We tend to attribute causality to the symptom we see rather than the disease that we don't. But it can be a serious error to not look deeper. And not just because we would miss a chance to engage the bigger issue. By interpreting the problem as arising from the location at which it shows up (here with Dubinsky) and not the one from which it originates (the executive suite), we keep the whole charade going. This is one reason why an identity crisis can be so debilitating.

The Fate of Donna Dubinsky

I always ask my classes what, in the end, is their final evaluation of Dubinsky. My underlying question is: How do you handle yourself when the purpose of the business is in question? Was Donna Dubinsky—hampered by an incomplete understanding of the intensifying upper-atmosphere conflict between Jobs and Sculley—confused and compromised by her own seemingly self-interested motives? Or had she also nonetheless managed to do the right thing? Had she penetrated and outed Apple's identity crisis at least enough to have unsettled its deepest underpinnings? We may not be able to answer this question definitively, but we can gain some insight by looking at what happened next to Dubinsky, as well as to Jobs and Sculley.

Late in the evening on Monday, April 22, 1985, Bill Campbell called Dubinsky as promised and, rather astonishingly, agreed to her request to be the sole decider of distribution strategy. He told her, "Take a month to do an analysis of the distribution process, and at the end of the month the executive staff will hear your recommendations."

Dubinsky obliged Campbell and delivered her analysis in late May. Somewhat anticlimactically, the executive staff signed off on her proposal. Campbell then called her again, once more with a surprise. He invited Dubinsky to suggest ways of reorganizing the business. And, as it happened, on June 14 a memorandum went out to the company from Sculley, outlining a plan to integrate R&D and manufacturing for all Apple product lines in a single division—uncannily, along much the same lines Dubinsky had recommended. At least in organizational terms, it signaled the end of a sibling rivalry between pirates and the navy. At the very least, it meant that the differences between the Mac and the Apple II lines could be rationally reconciled rather than being fought over in a deadly internal competition.

It is interesting to speculate how it came to pass that someone who, weeks earlier, was at risk of crashing and burning at Apple was now being asked to offer suggestions about how to realign the company.

What had made this possible? Although we don't have access to what Campbell and Sculley were thinking at the time, we do know, from recently published memoirs, what was happening simultaneously at the top of the organization. While the Dubinsky-Coleman drama was unfolding a couple of levels down from Steve Jobs and John Sculley, Apple's board was wrestling with the conflict at the top. Unbeknownst to Dubinsky, the battle over this unhealthy dynamic had erupted at Apple's board meeting on April 10—a week before her fateful confrontation with Sculley. Again, the words of former Apple exec Andy Hertzfeld:

"The conflict came to a head at the April 10th board meeting. The board thought they could convince Steve to transition back to a product visionary role, but instead he went on the attack and lobbied for Sculley's removal. After long, wrenching discussions with both of them, and extending the meeting to the following day, the board decided in favor of John, instructing him to reorganize the Macintosh division, stripping Steve of all authority."

Having lost his showdown with Sculley, Jobs stayed on at Apple for several more months, in a much-curtailed role. Then, on Friday, May 31, 1985, the board announced Jobs's removal, along with the first quarterly loss in the company's history. Hertzfeld said of the time, "It was surely one of the lowest points of Apple history."

The consonant events here are noteworthy. It seems clear that there were powerful replications of dynamics at the levels of strategy, senior leadership, and middle management. This leads us to an important hypothesis that we will explore in this book: Often, the complicated experiences we have with colleagues in our business, and the confusing political and personal machinations we encounter at every level, are likely not just ours alone but rather enactments of the larger, more central, problems in the business.

This gives additional credence to the earlier warning. There is an unfortunate tendency for executives to see a problem "down below" and attribute its cause to the place where the problem is expressed, as if one were to blame an illness on its symptoms.[4] But if Apple's distribution issue is any indication, attributing causality to the level where dysfunction is expressed may be a mistake and, moreover, may very well set up a vicious dynamic. Conflicts denied at the top of an organization flow through unseen channels to weak spots elsewhere in the business.

In short, if you're a leader, don't rush to see the symptom as the cause. If you came upon a woodland spring, you probably wouldn't conclude that you'd found its source right there at your feet; rather, you'd likely believe the actual source to be miles away. A similar approach is helpful in business.

The proxy war suggests an uncomfortable possibility. We are all unknowing players in unfolding dramas for which we rarely have the script. Although we tend to believe that we are the ones who manage the tensions in the business, perhaps a more accurate statement is that the tensions in the business manage us. Exchanges like the one between Dubinsky and Sculley may feel deeply personal, but they are also pathways by which the impersonal strategic issues in the business find their outlets.

One of the goals of this book is to enable leaders to understand and confront these latent dynamics, rather than becoming victim to them; to stop the drama from playing itself out over and over throughout the organization.

So what did become of Donna Dubinsky in the wake of Apple's crisis? She remained at Apple until 1991, when she left to become the CEO of Palm Computing, which ultimately produced the Palm Pilot—one of the earliest successful PDAs. She continued her career as an innovative force in the technology industry, most recently as cofounder and CEO of the software firm Numenta, which has developed a computing platform using algorithms modeled on the high-level functioning of the human brain. In 2007 she was given the Harvard Business School Alumni Achievement Award, the highest honor the school bestows on its graduates.

2

The Murky Middle

Homer's *Odyssey* tells the story of the Greek hero Odysseus making his ten-year journey home from the Trojan War to Ithaca, where his legendarily patient wife Penelope awaited his return. En route, Odysseus must pass by two great sea monsters flanking the Strait of Messina, between what is now Sicily and southern Italy. The first of the two monsters, Scylla, has six heads and twelve feet; it feeds on careless sailors who pass too closely. On the other side, rooted in the sea floor, is the monster Charybdis, whose gaping aperture causes whirlpools that swallow ships whole. The middle way being too narrow to pass without coming within range of one of the monsters, Odysseus faced the dilemma of choosing the "least worst option." His was the first case study of a basic leadership dilemma!

The word "dilemma," from the Greek, means "two premises." It applies when we face a choice between two alternatives, either of which is thought to be undesirable. For example, we often say that one is caught on the "horns of a dilemma." This usage of the term comes from Phaedrus, in the Socratic

Dialogues, who likened facing a dilemma to squaring off against a charging bull. To confront the bull, you can choose to risk either the right horn or the left. But either way, the bull is inescapable. The prospect of choosing which risk to accept can induce decision-making paralysis.

The heart of an organization's identity crisis is a dilemma. Understanding this dilemma is the first part of resolving the crisis. Failing to do so merely prolongs or exacerbates it, as shown by the following tragic story of the cable news network CNN.

CNN Faces a Crisis

In 1980, Cable News Network (CNN) was an audacious enterprise. Founded in the retrofitted basement of an Atlanta grocery store, CNN was the first all-news cable television channel. The company's identity was deeply rooted in the innovative niche it had created for itself. CNN's early journalists identified themselves as "news guerillas," pioneering a journalistic revolution. At CNN's helm was the colorful and outspoken Ted Turner. Turner wanted to bring something new into the world by bucking the mainstream news titans. Characterizing his strategy for covering news, Turner declared, "I am one of those do-gooders. If people don't watch the UN coverage this year, I am going to keep on running it. I am going to shove it down their throats."

For its first ten years, CNN was wildly successful. Even as colleagues in the mainstream networks joked about the "Chicken Noodle network's" humble grocery-store origins, CNN *had* revolutionized news. So significant was its impact that officials at the Pentagon coined the term "the CNN effect" to describe the consequences of real-time, twenty-four-hour coverage of government decision making. CNN had a found a galvanizing purpose in satisfying a powerful unmet need in the market: constant coverage of global events in an increasingly globalized world.

But by the mid-1990s, CNN's ratings fluctuated wildly as hot news stories came and went. Big events like the O. J. Simpson case gave CNN a lift, but only temporarily. It was a feast-or-famine business model, dictated by forces outside of CNN's control (see Figure 2.1).

Figure 2.1. Viewers Over Time by Network Show CNN's Dependence on Major News Events and the Precipitous Rise of Fox News

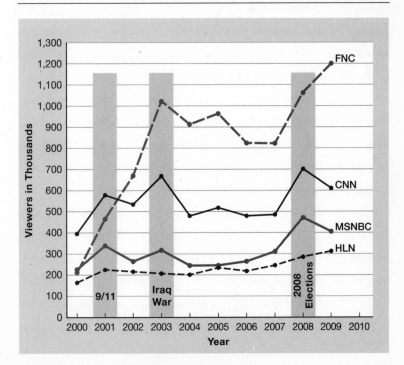

The early stirrings of dilemma would soon increase. By the late 1990s, the democratization of world news, which CNN helped make happen, flung the door wide open to the likes of Fox News and MSNBC, who brought new purposes and thus identities to the market. The upstart Fox had successfully grafted the personality-driven radio talk show format of shows like Rush Limbaugh's onto cable television, tailoring its programming to a growing conservative audience. MSNBC soon followed with a similar position for liberals.

It wasn't long before Fox News overtook CNN in the ratings. Audiences stopped tuning in for world events in places like Bosnia, Rwanda, Haiti, and North Korea. By CNN's twentieth anniversary, rival programs on MSNBC and Fox News—highly attuned to the appetites of their particular audiences—had waged a spirited and sustained challenge to CNN. Chief among the antagonists was Bill O'Reilly, who owned the all-important 8 PM slot, for which CNN had no answer. With O'Reilly at the helm, Fox's lead began to lengthen.

The dilemma that sets a crisis in motion often originates with industry changes, so it is important to unpack what happened in the news market. At CNN, technological disruption got the ball rolling. Prior to 1980, television news was relatively straightforward. Nationwide broadcast networks—NBC, CBS, and ABC—provided bare-bones reporting once or twice a day. By the 1980s, the new medium of cable had sparked an innovation: CNN introduced 24/7 coverage of world events by leveraging its ubiquitous global presence. Value migrated from NBC, CBS, and ABC to CNN. But CNN's democratizing of the news fertilized the field for the next innovation:

point-of-view-based news. Fox News and MSNBC went beyond the five W's—who, what, when, where, and why—to solve other problems for viewers. Value migrated once more, diluting CNN's original position.

To gain an appreciation for the changes in the news sector, refer to Figure 2.2, which depicts a simplified version of the process by which the categories in a market multiply in the wake of new innovation.[1] Disruptive technologies open the door for new problems-to-solve and thus new entrants. The market grows more complicated, the construction of firms' identities more nuanced, while the number of firm identities proliferates. Imagine, for example, adding one more level to the figure, encompassing the dense segmentations across news options in the digital medium. One could do similar exercises for other industries, from high tech to hospital systems. Given the profuse permutations of business models, media, and problems-to-solve, Ted Levitt's challenge about choosing what business you're in might seem quaint to the modern strategist.

Figure 2.2. The Evolution of the News Market Structure over Time Illustrates How Categories Become More Complicated over Time

	Medium		Problem-to-Solve			Players		
1950's–1980's	National Broadcast (Network)		5 W's			NBC, CBS, ABC		
1980's–1990's	Network	Cable	5 W's		24/7 + Global	NBC, CBS, ABC		CNN
1990's–2010	Network	Cable	5 W's	24/7 + Global	Political	NBC, CBS, ABC	CNN	FOX, MSN, BC

As technologies disrupt markets, new categories of opportunity emerge, putting pressure on companies to rethink their purposes.

Rethinking their purposes is exactly what happened at CNN. In response to Fox News and MSNBC, Walter Isaacson, then the head of CNN News, decided to tweak CNN's identity.[2] Isaacson recruited Connie Chung for the coveted 8 PM slot to compete with Fox. Instead of unapologetically reporting important world events regardless of their entertainment quotient, Isaacson and Chung ran a quasi-tabloid program that featured sensationalized stories (kidnappers and pedophiles being among the network's favorites) alongside traditional news. Initially, ratings rose. CNN received an additional boost from another major world event: the first Iraq War. Though the ratings issue temporally subsided, Chung's show provoked tensions within the network. Rank and file saw in Chung everything they believed was wrong with the network. Chasing ratings, they believed, had compromised CNN's journalistic principles and legacy. Privately, many staffers thought Chung was an embarrassment. As one staffer told a media reporter, "Some of us here are trying to do *real* journalism."

The tumult grew and then subsided. Isaacson left later that year, and his successor, Jim Walton, vowed to restore the focus on hard news. The period of confusion was over, Walton declared. In a highly symbolic act, he forced out Chung.

But that didn't solve the problem. The 8 PM slot remained open, and Fox continued to widen the gap. Walton wanted a change and was determined to escape the feast-or-famine cycle. When it came to making viewing decisions, Walton believed that "people watch people." To give the network a boost, he and senior CNN leadership reached out to a team of Hollywood veterans with experience in entertainment TV. They initiated a project, dubbed "TV 101," to teach CNN how to do deliver the news in a more entertaining way.

While Walton strategized, the 8 PM vacuum grew more urgent. Baghdad fell in April 2003, draining CNN ratings. Walton knew that audiences would soon return to their normal viewing habits, and CNN would have no answer to its flashier rivals. It was during this transition that Walton followed a hunch. If personalities sell, then why not look to one of CNN's most formidable on-air anchors? Paula Zahn ran the morning show with distinction. CNN's AM ratings had tripled since she joined the network. And she delivered the news straight, shunning the typical morning-show fare of cooking segments and lifestyle or entertainment spots. It was the perfect blend of personality and integrity.

Putting Zahn in the 8 PM slot may have made sense in theory, but Walton's strategy was awkwardly executed. The 8 PM position had originally been conceived as a one-hour slot in order to accommodate evening audiences' viewing habits. Walton expanded it, pulling Zahn's entire three-hour show into the slot—a feat no one had attempted before. But the show lacked the cadence, rhythm, and structure necessary to hold audience attention for three evening hours. It lurched from story to story. Worse, Zahn didn't go after the big news stories that many at CNN had hoped for. Instead, she served up dramatized pieces on the Laci Peterson case or a notorious hazing incident at Glenbrook North High School in Northbrook, Illinois. Mysteriously, Zahn eventually went on an unannounced—and indefinite—vacation.

The media world took notice. Tom Rosenstiel, the director of the Project for Excellence in Journalism, observed that Fox News "knew what it was doing and CNN didn't." Bill O'Reilly, rubbing salt in the wound, taunted CNN from his Fox News perch: "We're on a Paula alert? Where's Paula? Has anyone seen her?"

Desperate now, CNN considered every possibility to fill the 8 PM slot—including booking live musical performances for each show and hiring the aging rocker Neil Young as a roving musical reporter. Despite such manic experimentation, none of the options seemed to fit. As one staffer later recalled, "What became clear to all of us was that we were trying to put a square peg in a round hole."

One can interpret CNN's vacillation, experimentation, and naked desperation—played out around a single block of programming—as evidence of a deeper struggle within the network. Walton joined CNN espousing a return to hard news, but he then reversed direction with Zahn. Such inconsistencies and contradictions are signs of a brewing crisis. When a company behaves erratically—and in a manner at odds with its own espoused positions—there are usually deep fundamental tensions at work.

There were indeed such tensions at CNN, and they soon spread. As the battle played out in the marketplace, a geographic schism opened within CNN. The move toward big personalities like Chung and Zahn pulled the center of gravity of the network away from Atlanta and toward New York. Outsiders observed Atlanta employees casually deriding their New York colleagues as "the Burbank crowd," a riff on the New York unit's connections with Hollywood celebrities.

And the New York contingent called their southern CNN colleagues "inbred."

Over the next two years, CNN struggled to regain its place in the news world. There were occasional bursts of optimism. CNN received a prestigious Peabody Award for its outstanding coverage of the 2008 presidential election. It trounced Fox News and MSNBC in the election ratings, pulling in audiences the size of those two networks combined. The victory reminded the news world that people still went to CNN for serious broadcast journalism. Around the same time, CNN launched Campbell Brown's *No Bias, No Bull* in the 8 PM slot, a program billed as the "antidote to Bill O'Reilly." Shortly thereafter, the controversial (and right-leaning) Lou Dobbs resigned. It was a moment of seeming clarity.

It didn't last. Tensions flared anew. But this time there would be a little bit of theater.

In November 2005, CNN reporter Rick Sanchez insisted on receiving a jolt of fifty thousand volts from a police-issued stun gun live on TV. The reporter buckled, straightened himself, and shivered off the lingering current in his body, only to offer a terse and hardly newsworthy analysis of the controversial police deterrent: "It hurt," he said.

Sanchez's stunt—only one in a long line of his "experiential" reporting coups—went viral immediately. Jon Stewart aired the footage, running the clip at regular speed, then repeatedly—and painfully—in slow motion. The next day, Sanchez's own CNN colleague, Anderson Cooper, piled on, as did the CNN *American Morning* crew.

Despite the flak, Sanchez was undeterred, and five years later, as CNN celebrated its thirtieth anniversary, he was again the focal point of tension between news and entertainment. CNN executives had proposed taking a one-hour block away from Wolf Blitzer's *The Situation Room* and giving it to Sanchez's new show, *Rick's List*. The move ignited a firestorm at the network. As reported by Politico's Michael Calderone, at a CNN annual meeting with Walton in attendance, Howie Lutt, the senior director of Blitzer's show, stood and asked the two hundred people in attendance to raise their hands if they respected Blitzer as a journalist.[3] It must have been an awkward moment for staffers. Nevertheless, nearly every hand in the room went up. Lutt then asked the same question about Sanchez. Only a few hands rose.

Seen in context, Lutt's gambit was more than a parry in some minor bout over airtime between two programs. The Sanchez/Blitzer affair was really a key battle for the heart and soul of the network.

How had CNN lost its way? On one hand, the network was a serious news outlet that honored facts, did smart analysis, and covered big world events. On the other, in order to fend off competitors like Fox News and MSNBC, CNN had begun to experiment with a different kind of business characterized by bigger personalities, sensational news stories, opinion, and a little bit of theater. The problem was that these two identities expressed starkly incompatible purposes, each targeting different audiences with different products, derived through opposing values, core assets, processes, and cultures. And instead of laying claim to one position or the other, CNN clumsily experimented with both, drifting down a path one staffer dubbed "the murky middle."

CNN's tribulations demonstrate that the failure to choose derives from a dilemma. Like Odysseus, the network faced a choice between options that posed risks and potential losses. To wholeheartedly embrace traditional journalism, CNN would have had to risk losing viewers interested in alternative forms of news; conversely, adopting a Fox-like strategy would mean abandoning founder Ted Turner's vision of a no-stars network giving its audience the news they needed but might not always want. Rather than accept the tradeoffs required to go all-in on either position, CNN compromised, straddled, and oscillated between irreconcilable identities. Judging by its erratic behavior, the network's tactics weren't the product of reasoned decision making but an expression of lacking the *clarity needed to make a choice.*

It should be mentioned that in January 2013 Jeff Zucker was named the new president of CNN Worldwide. Zucker immediately promised to change CNN and differentiate the fabled news network from its competitors. We will see what he does.

It's Harder Than You Think

Business books are often cavalier in indicting business leaders for their "obvious mistakes." It would be easy to criticize CNN for its textbook case of an identity crisis. But the network's succession of presidents would surely tell a more complex and nuanced story. We might then see their indecisiveness not as a lack of nerve or sound business judgment but as a reasonable way to manage a strong set of cross-pressures that made the act of choosing especially difficult. Indeed, Isaacson, Walton, and other CNN leaders may have believed that they *were* choosing.

A fuller, clearer picture of what constitutes the identity crisis requires digging beneath the surface. We need some sympathy for the factors that make dilemmas so insoluble and choosing so bedeviling. We're not privy to the inner struggles of the leaders of CNN. But I can tell you the story of a company with which I do have firsthand experience—a groundbreaking digital marketing agency I'll call Dividio (a pseudonym used to protect their identity).

Dividio helps old-economy companies adapt to the new digital world. Chances are you've seen Dividio's work. The cool website you just visited, the pop-up in your browser window, or the mobile app that connects you to your favorite store are the kinds of things that Dividio does. They create technologies that enable brands to interact with customers in novel ways.

Founded by an intrepid band of entrepreneurs, Dividio survived celebrity success, the dot-com crash, the exit of its founders, and a number of mergers and acquisitions to become a highly respected professional-services firm. The agency— now a part of a larger media and marketing holding company called Stellar—has repeatedly earned a place on the list of best marketing agencies in the world. The stalwarts who survived the firm's early tribulations were running the business when it became a client of mine.

In 2009, I spent two days facilitating a Dividio leadership summit whose goals were to help the company's cadre of two dozen top leaders think about the business, its future, and the impact of any changes on their exercise of leadership. At the end of the second day, after a stretch of long conversations about strategy, I asked participants to jot down on a piece of paper their reflections about the business and their discussions that day. Here is what they wrote:

"The lack of clarity right now is exhausting." ✶

"We, the group in the room, are not clear on the positioning. How do we expect the rest of the company to be?"

"We need to continue to push for a common language. We spend a lot of time debating issues that are based on semantics or assumptions rather than dealing with issues clearly and commonly."

"Our lack of a defined position in the market helped us in the past but will hurt us in the future."

"If we don't pull together and operate from a common strategic framework, we are done—and our heritage of decentralization is biting us in the ass."

"Our company needs a new, simple narrative."

"We have to make hard decisions that are unpopular, difficult, and discriminatory."

These comments are vehement. They are urgent. Along with their frustration and impatience, you sense Dividio's leaders yearning for clarity. This is because, more than anything else, they care. Their words reveal an unmistakable desire to *do something*. But what, exactly? And what is it that they find so unclear? How should that lack of clarity be addressed?

It seemed to me that the leaders were talking about purpose. Their sense of urgency arose from the feeling that they'd lost their way. They'd lost sight of the essential North Star that would align all the aspects of the business. Dividio's leaders were aching for a choice to be made. And as we saw with CNN, restoring purpose and making a choice would require breaking through a paralyzing dilemma.

When my colleagues and I began working with Dividio, we encountered a company buffeted in the crosscurrents of conflicting ideas about what it wanted to be. Imagine a company pulled in opposing directions across two axes, each of which represent a core question about the business. The first axis was the question of whether Dividio was an advertising agency or a consulting firm—two identities that differ in many important respects. An advertising agency provides creative marketing to clients using digital technology; think of a company running an advertising campaign over Facebook or Twitter. A consulting firm, by contrast, designs and builds technology that helps clients generate more value for their customers; imagine here an e-commerce platform that enables customers to access content or purchase things online. The focus of the former is advertising, branding, and marketing; the latter, strategy and enabling transactions. Dividio was torn between those two identities.

The second axis was the question of whether Dividio should be a specialist or a "lead agency." In Dividio's universe, a specialist takes someone else's idea—whether that be a big marketing campaign from an ad agency or a strategic initiative for a new platform from the client—and executes it. As a specialist, Dividio is expert at building content, functionality, and value in the digital world. But it does so primarily by following a recipe created by someone else.

A lead agency, by contrast, is a full-service provider. It both conceives and executes strategy. As a lead agency, Dividio would create the big ideas *and* execute them, and it would do so across all media in both the online and the offline world. If the specialist is the strong supporting role, the lead agency is the writer and director.

As a way to surface the ambivalence on these issues during the leadership summit, we used a simple tool called the Strategic Options Questionnaire, created by the Center for Applied Research (CFAR), the firm I was working with at the time. For each of the two axes, we asked the twenty-four leaders to characterize the *present* state of the company and what they believed it should become in the *future*.

The results were revealing. The group largely believed they were headed toward becoming—or aspired to be—a lead agency. However, they were much more conflicted about whether Dividio was, and ought to become, a consulting firm or an ad agency.

The results of the survey stimulated a provocative but uncomfortable conversation. I remember vividly one senior leader reacted strongly to the lack of clarity. "We don't take a stand in the world of agencies or in the world of consultancies," he said. "We are unwilling to make a choice or think about the implications of choosing a direction. These big choices hang over the business but are never made. As a result, a lot of incompatible activities can continue claiming to be high priorities, and the organization pulls against itself."

Stimulated by the data, participants fitfully debated the two questions for a while before giving up on the conversation. Everyone in the room had a vague sense that the identity of the business was changing, but there was no consensus on what that change should be. After about forty-five minutes, only one thing had become clear: the group found talking about these issues almost unbearable.

This kind of impasse is common. In my experience, every organization struggles over different versions of what to be. As a way to appreciate the dynamics, think about your own company. Lurking beneath the surface are likely opposing tensions around what your organization is or ought to be. What are your own versions of "specialist versus lead agency"? If you can locate the opposing positions, take a step further. Between the two options you identified, where would you locate your company at the present? How about eighteen months from now? Would your colleagues agree with your assessment? Going further, what would be the impact on your organization if employees worked from divergent or confusing understandings of the business?

All businesses have their internal contradictions and disagreements, but Dividio had been supporting materially different concepts of the business for some time. As Dividio grew over the years, it had taken on different kinds of work. It had begun to move, however sporadically, from being a niche role player to being a quasi-lead agency, but it was still far from reaching lead status. It had one or two large clients with whom the company legitimately felt it was in the lead, but for the majority of others Dividio provided purely specialist work. Similarly, Dividio bounced back and forth between performing types of work characteristic of either an agency or a consultancy. Indeed, some clients saw Dividio as an advertising agency, others as a consulting firm.

For a while, the balancing act among these four identities felt sustainable. Dividio could manage to be many things to many people. This wasn't necessarily efficient, or purposeful, but the strategy enabled Dividio to generate work in good times and bad. And the company thrived and developed a reputation for producing great work. Moreover, because the market for digital services hadn't yet congealed, it was easy to argue that a robust, bifurcated identity could appeal to different audiences. But being many things to many people successfully couldn't last forever.

Market Moves

As with CNN, the latent confusion at Dividio was brought to a head by changes in the market. The shifting structure of the industry began to force Dividio's hand. Those changes precipitated the crisis and made the call for choice all the more urgent.

It's helpful to consider the remarkable impact that market changes can have on a company's identity. As we saw with CNN, purposes and identities of businesses are linked to the structures of the markets in which they compete. Problems-to-solve emerge as the market evolves.

As an illustration, consider beer. Between the end of Prohibition and 1995, large commercial breweries like Anheuser-Busch and Miller gobbled up hundreds of smaller breweries. As the number of commercial beer companies declined, so did the variety and flavor of the beer—its biodiversity, if you will. That left little room for noncommercial tastes. The market had become homogenized. But then something interesting happened. In 1979 President Carter deregulated the industry, unleashing pent-up demand for alternatives to commercial beer (see Figure 2.3). Suddenly, there was a new problem-to-solve in the market.

Figure 2.3. The Rise of Craft Beers in America

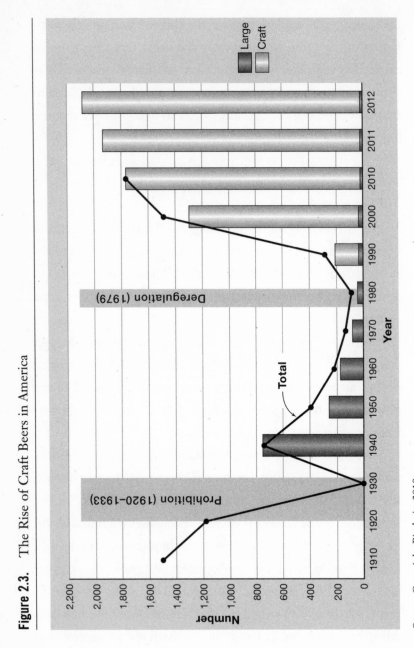

Source: Copyright Biodesic, 2010.

As microbreweries rushed in to fill this void, these so-called craft brews developed purposes and identities very different from those of their commercial counterparts. Commercial beers were industrial; crafts were artisanal. Commercial beers all tasted the same; craft beers showcased an exceedingly diverse range of complex flavors. Commercial beers emphasized their national presence; crafts were regional. And so on and so forth.

Few markets are so simply structured as the beer industry, but the evolution in brewing illustrates a common pattern: fluctuations in market categories tend to stimulate new problems-to-solve. New problems thereby give rise to new purposes, and new purposes to new identities. The latter consequence occurs because purpose is defining; it fashions a particular kind of identity for the company. Artisanal, flavorful, regional—these defining characteristics emerged as craft breweries fulfilled their purpose as an alternative to commercial beers.

We see a similar but more complex process unfold with Dividio. Just as deregulation triggered ferment in the beer industry, technology drove disruptions in digital advertising. After the birth of the Web, ad agencies came in roughly two different types: traditional firms that created big advertising campaigns via television, print, and radio; and digital agencies, which specialized in advertising on the Internet.

For a time, a firewall neatly separated traditional and digital agencies. Traditional firms didn't do digital, and digital firms didn't do traditional media or develop creative. These distinctions were as much about self-image as they were about strategic position. The upstart digital agencies in New York's

Flatiron district could thumb their noses at the Madison Ave. types who, in turn, pretended they didn't care—after all, they had the ear of the chief marketing officer and, in effect, owned the client.

But by the mid-2000s, the division of labor in the marketplace began to blur. Two shifts precipitated the erosion of the firewall between traditional and digital.

First, digital simply became the dominant medium for advertising. Consumers began spending about as much time online as they did watching TV or listening to the radio. And in the digital space advertisers could do things that were impossible in print or on TV. For example, they could interact with users and capture deep insights about them based on their online activity. Content creators in the digital realm also moved beyond conveying just the right ideas or messages to designing "unique user experiences." Practically speaking, digital channels enabled marketers to entice consumers, in real time, to make an online purchase. The effectiveness of alternate design and creative options for digital channels could be measured and tweaked on the fly. For print and TV? Not so much.

Parity between traditional and digital media allowed digital agencies to play a bigger role both in setting advertising and marketing strategy for clients, and in coming up with the big ideas.

Second, the number of media channels proliferated. Where once there were only traditional media and relatively static web pages, now there are smartphones, tablets, social media sites like Twitter and Facebook, businesses' crowdsourcing portals, pushed and pulled texting applications, location-aware (GPS-enabled) marketing—and whatever else is new this week and clamors for a strategy. The diversity of channels made the distinctions between traditional and digital media less meaningful. Instead, marketers needed the dexterity to deliver compelling campaigns and content across *all* channels. They needed tight integration and someone who could take the lead across different forms of media.

The blurring of lines led to a horse race between traditional and digital agencies. As of this writing, that race is still on. Digital firms aspire to usurp the place of their creative counterparts as lead agencies. Traditional firms are gunning to acquire the technical chops of interactive agencies to create and execute in the digital realm. All are converging on the same turf from different starting points.

These market shifts have created a critical choice point for larger digital shops. As the firewall falls, they have to choose whether to enter the race to be lead agency or accept a narrower specialist role. Dividio had to ask itself: Does this company want to be a best-of-breed specialist or an agency that can do it all? The two options are largely incommensurate, implying different business models, customers, skill sets, and cultures.

A Hard Choice

After the summit, we began working with a small group of Dividio leaders to see whether progress could be made on their vision. The leaders gave us an updated version of their strategy to review. To our surprise, the document hinted at one big decision: they seemed to have embraced marketing as the focus of the business and "agency" as their core identity (and dropped the idea of being a consultancy). It was a weak embrace, but a good start. The specialist/lead agency question, on the other hand, was left unresolved.

As a springboard for the discussion, we drafted a short memo that laid out the key choices and described why failing to answer them could harm the business. We suggested that Dividio had been paralyzed by the choices it faced—and that it might be productive to confront them head-on.

The small group included Paul, the North American president; Mark, the vice president of strategy; and Laura, the vice president of human resources.

Stimulated by our note, the group moved quickly to the heart of the matter. Paul, Mark, and Laura could see that choosing to become a lead agency would have enormous implications, both for Dividio's senior leaders and for its relationship with its parent company, Stellar. But they couldn't say yes *or* no to the lead agency role. The resources required would drain short-term financials.

Nor could the group envision saying yes *or* no to the specialist role. To say yes would mean becoming a bit player in the industry and staking out the company's position in what was fast becoming a commoditized service. Choosing the specialist role would mean consciously stepping back from the potential to grab for the brass ring. Of all the digital agencies in the world, Dividio was seen by industry leaders as having many of the necessary pieces to move up to the lead-agency position. As with Phaedrus's charging bull, neither of the options felt good.

It's worth showing you how Paul, Mark, and Linda wrestled with this difficult dilemma because the underlying dynamics are the central driver of the story.

"Honestly," Laura began, "we would have to accept a lot of sacrifice to choose the lead agency role."

Paul agreed: "The three regions haven't invested in the capabilities needed to build a lead agency. They are poorly positioned to make the move."

"I wonder whether the regional heads would accept that the choice we're talking about is even real," added Mark. "We don't like to talk about the specialist versus lead agency because we don't want to admit that there *is* a choice."

"We don't say that out loud," added Paul.

Laura was struck by Mark's comment. "What do you mean?" she asked.

"Maybe we've *already* chosen the specialist route," explained Mark. "It's a decision that's implicitly been made, but one that we're not willing to accept."

"If we *have* made that decision," said Laura, "then we did it by default! Whatever we do—specialist or lead agency—I want it to be conscious, not some *fait accompli*. That's why we're talking right now!"

A member of Dividio's rank and file watching this conversation unfold would have found Mark's comment and Laura's vehement reaction revealing. Mark believed the organization was denying the fact that they really *are* specialists. By suppressing the reality of the choice between lead agency and specialist, every part of the business could go on *thinking* whatever it wanted ("We're an agency that does innovative and creative work") while *doing* something different ("We execute on other people's ideas"). Laura saw this duplicity as tragic for the company. To her, denying the choice was simply unacceptable.

By that point, Paul was staring down at the table. "The problem I'm struggling with isn't how we would execute either option," he said. "I am struggling with the choice itself."

Paul said he felt that the business couldn't meet its near-term financial performance targets and at the same time build the agency of the future—"The two things aren't compatible." He also argued that the long-term investment plan that Stellar had recently established for Dividio's forty most-senior leaders was part of the problem. Its incentives tied the executives' compensation to specific revenue and margin targets *over the next thirty months*. Because the lead agency role would require cutting back on specialist work while simultaneously making big investments in new talent, the shift in strategy would jeopardize everyone's compensation.

As if weighed down by the prospect of rallying his autonomous regional leaders behind the choice, Paul put two objections on the table: Not only would a shift to the lead agency role infringe on the regions' traditional autonomy, but initiating the change would make the lucrative new incentives unachievable. "If we don't choose right, those forty people could lose a lot of money." *That* was the dilemma.

Laura countered by asking Paul to take the long view: "I sensed at the summit a burning passion to do something great. The ultimate bummer is that our way of operating around here is to react to things, but not push for doing something important."

Mark broke in: "But people don't recognize how different a company we would have to be!"

The three then fell into a heavy silence. At the time it felt interminable. Paul finally spoke: "I've been thinking lately that maybe *I'm* the problem. I'm the person between Stellar and the regional heads. The group of people interested in [becoming a] lead agency may be the minority. Maybe it's *me* who needs to come around."

At this point, Paul, Laura, and Mark were all depressed. At our urging, Paul decided to give it one more try and speak with both his leadership team and Stellar's management. We heard back from him two weeks later. Paul said he had a new plan, though it wasn't much different from the original.

Two weeks later, Paul left Dividio.

Paul had faced a dilemma. He could have tried to push his regional leaders to rally around a forward-thinking lead agency position—despite knowing that they were incented against embracing that move. He would have had to put all of his leadership capital on the line, knowing that the chances of prevailing were slim. Or he could have negotiated with Stellar to loosen the constraints of the long-term investment plan and accept that Dividio would need to make near-term investments in new skills while also putting expected revenues at risk. To Paul, both options presented insurmountable obstacles. He was anguished over what to do.

Paul's anguish rightly brings us back to Odysseus, whose voyage through the Strait of Messina required that he choose between two deadly monsters. Odysseus' dilemma—like Paul's—was not so different from those that many executives face. However, they do not always heed the lesson embedded in this 2,800-year-old tale. Odysseus was forced to accept the inevitable risk and loss that came bundled with the act of making a clear decision. He opted to pass close to Scylla, thereby losing only a few of his sailors, rather than risk losing his whole ship and crew to Charybdis.

It is easy to imagine Paul at the helm of a ship heading into the Strait of Messina. He sees the waiting monsters and feels the heavy burden of jeopardy they present. Can you easily say that you wouldn't have done as Paul did—changing course rather than choosing between Scylla and Charybdis?

Core dilemmas are deep and complicated phenomena. We must not underestimate the weight of the choices that fall on leaders' shoulders. Paul felt keenly his duty toward colleagues whose compensation would be put at risk by the change in strategy. At the heart of his consternation was a compelling human problem—one that appears to have kept him from playing the long-term strategic game. Instead, it became a reason *not* to choose—a near-term distraction that would stand in the way (as Laura observed) of "doing something important" for the business.

Odysseus, too, was pained by the prospect of putting his crew in harm's way. After all, they had fought together for years, defeated Troy, and Odysseus knew them all as brothers and friends. But he was nonetheless able to choose the "least worst option"—the one that would prevent the destruction of the ship—because he never lost sight of the journey's purpose: to get back home to Ithaca.

Leaders confront many powerful dynamics that can distract them from choosing a clear enterprise purpose. In the next chapter, you will learn more about the performance penalties that a murky identity imposes. It is very expensive to be neither fish nor fowl. No matter the short-term pain, it is always better to choose.

3

Neither Fish Nor Fowl

John F. Kennedy is said to have described the camel as "a horse designed by a committee." Leaving aside any slight on camels—which are beautifully evolved for their native climate—Kennedy wanted to make a point about the way committees make decisions. His point, which relates to a core problem explored in this book, is that organized efforts to satisfy competing agendas typically end up pleasing no one.

This is as true in business as it is in politics, architecture, or any number of other fields. A business can be one thing or another but will invariably suffer when it tries to be too many things at once. The unsatisfying in-between state of being "neither fish nor fowl" is likely to incur a variety of penalties. As we'll see, these penalties are paid internally as a cost to operational performance and also externally to the detriment of your brand in the market. As a general rule, consumers and other stakeholders shun things that defy preexisting categories or fail to stand out clearly on their own. We don't like things that confuse us.

A House Divided Cannot Stand

There is only so much tension an organization can bear without tearing itself apart. Abraham Lincoln observed that "a house divided against itself cannot stand." This applies to business as well. An organization pulled among competing purposes risks discord, fragmentation, and inefficiency. Companies that divide their attention and resources between competing purposes are, in effect, pulling their punches, applying half-hearted energy and focus to what should be fully committed activities. Over time, splitting the difference becomes a strategy unto itself—and not a very good one.

One of the best illustrations of a house divided and its impact on performance is the squaring off between Southwest and Continental airlines told by strategist Michael Porter.[1] One almost tires of hearing about Southwest as a business case. But they deserve the attention. The airline has had thirty-nine years of profitability in an industry where profits are excruciatingly difficult to earn. Almost more remarkable, the company has not laid off employees since the start of the recession in 2007. There's a simple reason why Southwest endures. The company has made a commitment.

Back in the 1990s, Southwest carved out a new space in the airline market by offering short-haul, low-cost, no-frills service to price-sensitive travelers. Southwest achieved this position by aligning all of its operational activities toward economy and volume. The airline eliminated meals, seating assignments, and first-class sections, and used automated ticketing to expedite throughput and bypass travel agencies that charged a commission for booking flights. Southwest used a single model of aircraft, which remains a hallmark of the company today. In a June 2012 interview with *Slate* magazine's Seth Stevenson, Southwest's vice president of ground operations, Chris Wahlenmaier, expounded on the benefits of operating a single aircraft:

> We only need to train our mechanics on one type of airplane. We only need extra parts inventory for that one type of airplane. If we have to swap a plane out at the last minute for maintenance, the fleet is totally interchangeable—all our on-board crews and ground crews are already familiar with it. And there are no challenges in how and where we can park our planes on the ground, since they're all the same shape and size.[2]

At Southwest all these reinforcing activities, from the seating procedures to plane selection, ensured fast turnarounds at the gate, making it possible for Southwest to keep more planes in the air, increase the number of flights, and drive down ticket prices. Southwest's portfolio of activities all came together coherently to enhance the airline's ability to provide value in the low-cost space. The airline had a clear purpose that went far beyond a marketing slogan; it showed up in everything the company did. Purpose, decision making, and operational capabilities were tightly aligned.

Enticed by Southwest's success in the 1990s, Continental developed its own version of the low-cost model, which it called "Continental Lite." Like Southwest, Continental Lite eliminated meals and first-class services. As anticipated, these measures increased the speed of departures and lowered fares. But the airline soon encountered turbulence, figuratively speaking. Continental continued to maintain a full-service offering on all of its mainline routes. The airline's core business constrained the flexibility of its "Lite" sibling even as the new service weakened the core. Continental's full-service segment couldn't afford to drop travel agents or revamp its seat-assignment processes, nor could it offer the same frequent-flyer benefits to customers paying the Lite segment's lower fares.

To manage these contradictions, Continental compromised. The company lowered commissions for travel agents and watered down the frequent-flyer program across all service classes. But in attempting to compromise between two incompatible models, Continental failed to fully deliver on either purpose. The compromises produced inefficiencies in both service segments. The results were devastating. Late flights, cancellations, and angry customers cost Continental hundreds of millions of dollars—and the CEO his job.

Continental's misstep is a reminder that businesses succeed not in their parts but as a whole. Designed around a very clear purpose, to which it was committed, Southwest operated a holistic business that aligned a number of reinforcing, amplifying activities. Continental cherry-picked some of those Southwest-style activities. But the unity and alignment of activities around a focal purpose is what matters. The hybrid Southwest-style model was in conflict with Continental's core operation. Straddling these two positions eroded the efficiency of the business as a whole and its ability to generate value for customers seeking low-cost air travel. Clarity and alignment create value; confusion and compromise destroy it.

Data from a number of places shows us that companies that align around a unifying focus do better. Working with years of data from private-equity deals and other research, Chris Zook has made a compelling case that companies that pursue growth through their core business do remarkably better than those that attempt to build multiple cores or diversify.[3] He finds, for example, that private-equity companies achieve their best financial results acquiring neglected and underperforming businesses that are marooned within diversified conglomerates and then sharpening their business's focus. Similarly, acquisitions that expand the scale of the core business are twice as successful as those that diversify or expand scope.

Paradoxically, growth is likelier to come from focus—by narrowing rather than expanding scope. Companies that seek growth by stretching beyond their core don't often fare well. Zook writes, "It is almost as if most growth strategies harbor a dark, destructive force that causes companies to reduce their focus on their core business and thereby to depart from the basis of their real differentiation." We certainly see this in the Continental case. When Continental aped Southwest's positioning, it opened itself to distraction and contradiction. It strayed from its core—and paid a steep price.

There is a caveat here worth mentioning. The explosion of thinking on disruption and business model innovation has demonstrated that having a core purpose does not mean forever maintaining the status quo. Companies do and should reinvent themselves. But there is a big difference between redefining your purpose and attempting to stitch together conflicting business models. For this reason, the biggest dilemma in strategy right now is how companies can build the business of the future without destroying the business of today. As we'll see later, attempting to simultaneously preserve and replace the core is very likely a fool's errand. There is only so much artful balancing a company can endure. The goal of achieving balance between contradictory models often becomes the biggest excuse for failing to make the bigger choice.

Laws of Attraction and Aversion

My wife, Elizabeth, is completing her Ph.D. in sociology. During the first two years of her coursework, she would sometimes come home from class talking in a starstruck manner about this certain professor. Curious to understand what made this particular professor so compelling, I once asked her, "Why is this guy more interesting than the others?"

She thought for a bit and said simply, "He has a point of view."

A lot of what we call charisma in other people is really our response to their authentic points of view—the solid positions from which they operate and interpret the world. People who have a point of view are attractive because when they take a stand it expresses something that is integral to who they are. This stand makes them intelligible and coherent to the world. We rally around such people and place a high value on them— perhaps especially so in an era of expediency and opportunism, in which we may not know exactly where many people stand. We respect the fact that there is no disconnect between what they say and how they live. Although the personalities of such people may be complex and nuanced, as expressions of character their actions are purposeful, clear, and consistent.

The attractiveness of a point of view also applies to the way we think about businesses and brands. Markets reward

Figure 3.1. The "U-Curve" Displays the Hypothetical Relationship Between Market Positions in the Grocery Sector

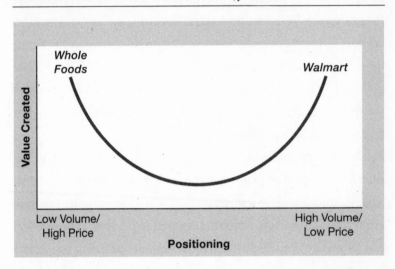

clarity of purpose and tend to punish ambiguity. Indeed, a central theme we have pursued thus far is simply this: clarity of purpose creates value; confusion destroys it.

To illustrate this principle, imagine for a moment the grocery industry and two of its most iconic brands: Whole Foods and Walmart. In Figure 3.1, I have placed these two firms on either end of a continuum. The left side of the continuum represents a low volume/high price position, and the right a high volume/low price position. The middle part of the continuum represents all positions in between. On the vertical axis is the amount of value created by these positions.

What we have is a U-shaped curve that starts high, drops low, and rises again. Whole Foods and Walmart are positioned at the two peaks of this curve. On the left, Whole Foods distinguishes itself from rivals by selling organic and gourmet foodstuffs. As its "Whole Paycheck" nickname sardonically implies, the Texas-based company competes primarily on margins they earn selling upscale foodstuffs. To the right, the mega retailer Walmart occupies a different market position by solving a very different problem. Walmart caters to a far larger base of customers—carrying a wider selection of household goods, electronics, and clothing items—and as a grocer, it competes on price. The business model depends on smaller margins, but larger volumes.

Both firms, it's safe to say, have staked out relatively distinctive high-value positions in the grocery sector. Walmart and Whole Foods occupy the peaks on the graph. I would argue that their value derives from two sources. The first is the alignment in their business model among the customer needs they satisfy, their particular value proposition, and their economic model. The second source of value is the clarity that each company achieves in the marketplace with its customers and other stakeholders. Most of us implicitly understand Whole Foods and Walmart without too much effort. Each business achieves its purposes distinctively, in a way that is recognizable and intelligible. It is as if their peaks rise prominently above the clouds. They know what they are and what they're about. And *only because of that* do we consumers know what they do and, therefore, when and why we should go to either one.

What then happens between the peaks? That's where things get murky. The idea behind the graph is that a company cannot successfully try to be both fish and fowl. It has to choose. When companies drift into the gulch between two distinct and intelligible market positions, they dilute value—both for customers and for the business. In the Introduction,

Figure 3.2. CNN's Drift into the "Murky Middle"

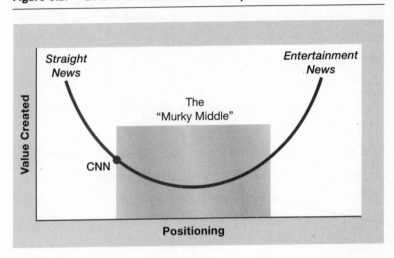

I described the problem Walmart encountered when it tried mixing higher-margin products into its "always low prices" strategy. What happened? The company got dinged by its customers because it had drifted into the murky middle.

CNN (Figure 3.2) is another good example. The network straddled the line between providing straight coverage of world events and personality-driven programing that sometimes veered into entertainment. Pressured by new market developments, CNN drifted between those two peaks in a kind of no-man's-land in the market structure. This is the dreaded murky middle, the space between clear purposes. It is the territory where underperforming companies can be found.

The operational side of things is half the story. Clarity involves more than efficiently executing your strategy or aligning your business. It is also about branding and intelligibility—the way the market perceives you as you do whatever it is you've chosen to do. To amplify this point, I want to introduce two concepts. The first, cognitive fluency, is drawn from psychology; the second, categorical imperative, from sociology. Together, they help explain how consumers decode and respond to clarity and confusion in the market.

Cognitive Fluency

One reason why markets reward clarity and punish ambiguity is quite simple: people respond better to things that are easy to think about and avoid those that are harder to make sense of. Ambiguity makes people work; it has what psychologists call "low cognitive economy." The more effort it takes to make sense of something, the less valid it seems. Clarity, on the other hand, is comforting. It enhances consumer confidence, helping prospective buyers evaluate whether an item being offered is good or bad. The preference for easy thinking is what psychologists refer to as "cognitive fluency." We might simplify this bias to the formula Easy = True.[4]

During the 2009 Super Bowl, a commercial that ran during halftime grabbed my attention. The shot panned across a number of people against a black backdrop. Some of the featured individuals like Dwyane Wade and Serena Williams, I recognized as celebrity athletes, even though they wore their street clothes. I also recognized Bill Russell, the great Boston Celtic. But many people I just couldn't place, including a young boy who couldn't have been older than twelve. Was he an athlete, I wondered? As the camera glided by, celebrities gazed intently into the lens while a voice-over offered cryptic observations about life and obliquely referenced something called "G." The final shot was of a group of masked street mimes.

The commercial, it turned out, was for Gatorade. It was an evocative piece, but puzzling to watch, particularly given the context. At no other time of the year do TV commercials get more scrutiny than during the Super Bowl. And many people, including me, found the G ad deeply confusing. Many viewers couldn't make the connection between G and Gatorade. Others were baffled by the juxtaposition of themes and characters.

Later I learned the backstory of the G campaign. Gatorade had been rebranded by PepsiCo. The once straightforward Gatorade had been replaced by the enigmatic G. Flavors like Orange Citrus and Berry had been renamed "No Excuses," "Be Tough," "Bring It," and "Shine On." People didn't get the new identity. According to *Beverage Digest*, after the Super Bowl ad aired Gatorade's volume fell by nearly 18 percent, and the brand lost four market share points in the second half of the year.[5]

What happened? You can see that the story is eerily similar to others I've been telling. The industry was changing. Driven by the ascendency of rivals like Powerade and by the rising popularity of fortified flavored-water drinks outside of the sports-drink category—like Vitamin Water—Gatorade felt compelled to expand its brand to appeal to nonathletes. To that end, even the athletes featured in the Super Bowl commercial were removed from the sporting context. The result was an ambiguous hybrid of old and new positions. The G brand's launch had decidedly low cognitive fluency.

Fortunately for Gatorade, the confusion was short-lived. Customers rebelled, and six months later the ad campaign was dropped by PepsiCo (though it would retain the "G" brand). By February of 2010, the company had revitalized its focus on athletic performance by introducing the G-Series—three new beverages designed to hydrate athletes before, during, and after strenuous exercise. The brand rebounded.

The Gatorade moment of confusion was much less severe than those of CNN and Continental, but it shows how easily companies can drift into the murky middle. It also shows how identity confusion can violate the natural human preference for cognitive fluency. Again, people grant more validity to offerings that they can more easily understand. For example, frivolous though this may seem, shares in companies with easy-to-pronounce names significantly outperform those with hard-to-pronounce names. The reverse is also true: when customers encounter ambiguous offerings that require more cognitive effort, they grant them lower validity. As Adam Alter, a psychologist at the Stern School of Business, puts it, "Every purchase you make, every interaction you have, every judgment you make can be put along a continuum from fluent to disfluent." Whether or not we are conscious of it, fluency influences judgment.[6]

The Categorical Imperative

Companies that ambiguously straddle different positions also violate what economic sociologists often refer to as the *categorical imperative* (not to be confused with a framework for moral behavior, by the same name, developed by the philosopher Immanuel Kant): consumers make judgments about the value of a company by referencing things they already understand—established market categories.

Market categories are everywhere. They are the background gestalt to our purchasing decisions. We instinctively know the difference between a Walmart and a Whole Foods, a Dell and an Apple, a Mercedes and a Ford, not just because of the properties of the products themselves but also by the different needs these companies satisfy. In the car sector, for example, there are very specific fundamental categories— luxury, economy, hybrid, and so on—that help us organize our choices as consumers. They make the options intelligible. The *categorical imperative* decrees that offerings that straddle categories or fall outside of the market's classification system are discounted because ambiguous offerings can't be easily evaluated against alternatives.[7]

Data is beginning to confirm the effect of the categorical imperative across industries. Studies illustrate that economic entities—ranging from individual movie actors and music artists to large corporations—underperform compared with their rivals if they don't fit within the market's customary taxonomy. For example, actors who can be easily typecast tend to find more work than their perhaps more brilliant but idiosyncratic peers.[8]

Personally, I was troubled by the premise that entities must conform to categories, especially in markets such as music and the arts, where I had hoped value might be placed on categorical innovation. Curious, I put the matter to an actor friend of mine. After thinking for a moment, he agreed. "The sad fact is that there are maybe one or two Daniel Day Lewises in a

generation who can play across roles, but the rest of us can't."
Indeed, he suggested, the exception proves the rule. For every
Daniel Day Lewis there are hundreds of artists whose careers
must obey the categorical imperative.

Making the Leap

Like any good rule, the categorical imperative is made to be
broken under the right conditions. When your product—
or the very identity of your company—has the potential to
become a category all its own, the categorical imperative seems
to break down. These successful deviations tell us a lot about
how consumer markets work, and, paradoxically, they support,
rather than weaken, the argument about clarity.

Consider the work of Harvard Business School Professor
Youngme Moon. In her 2011 book *Different: Escaping the Competitive Herd*, Moon argues that great companies build brand
identities that create a *meaningful difference* between themselves and others in the market. These companies separate
themselves from the herd by redefining the boundaries of the
market. The word "meaningful" here is important. Although
Moon gives no specific criteria for what distinguishes a *meaningful* difference from, say, a *negligible* one, she communicates
through her examples that some differences matter more than
others. We might say that a *meaningful* difference enables a
company to rise above the murky middle and achieve a new
peak in the market landscape. Twenty-four-hour cable news
didn't exist before Ted Turner launched CNN. Before its
lamentable descent into the murky middle, CNN had estab-

lished a vast meaningful difference between themselves and the traditional networks.

One of Moon's most persuasive examples of meaningful difference is the MINI Cooper first made by British Motor Corporation and now BMW. As a rule, Americans love big cars and trucks. They will typically not buy a small car if they can afford a larger one. Nonetheless, in 2002, when the MINI Cooper entered the American market, the company did a profoundly counterintuitive thing. Rather than downplay the car's diminutive proportions, marketers did just the opposite. To launch the car, BMW developed a cleverly self-aware advertising campaign that made a virtue of the MINI's stature. Billboards showed a picture of the distinctive new car and ran the following copy:

XXL   XL   M   S   MINI.

The campaign struck a chord with Americans. It helped the MINI Cooper stand out from the crowd as a fresh alternative. Moon argues that the car succeeded by making a meaningful difference in the market. To Moon's thesis we would add that by presenting such a stark contrast to alternatives, the MINI also embodied the clarity principle. There was absolutely nothing ambiguous about this car.

But hadn't the MINI Cooper also violated the categorical imperative? Yes and no. It certainly didn't straddle categories, but neither did it heed them. Most people buy compact cars for fuel economy and price. By comparison, the MINI Cooper was all about fun, with its sporty performance and quirky, innovative design. The combination of fun, high-concept design, and quality was uncharacteristic of the compact car space. In Youngme Moon's happy sense of the word, it was *meaningfully different*. By rejecting the homogenous confines of the compact car category, the MINI created a bold identity *of its own* in the market. It became a new peak on the market horizon.

This brings me back to the importance of choosing. As a kid I loved spending time at a lake in the summer. When my friends and I tired of sunning or waterskiing, we'd investigate the lake's many tree-lined coves looking for good rope swings. Most swings hung from a tree that bent far over the lake, the stout rope tied to a well-positioned branch. Like many child-hood activities, rope-swinging could be treacherous. To clear the rocks and tree stumps jutting up out of the shallow water, you had to attain escape velocity. This was not for the faint of heart. You had to climb to higher ground some distance back from the shore. And you had to go all in. A half-hearted leap would put you on the rocks. A successful (and safe) leap depended on your commitment to the leap.

This was the challenge that Continental faced and failed to meet. In a sense, it was also the obstacle the MINI Cooper faced and overcame. Every company must decide what it is and then *be* it—completely and unambiguously. Continental was half-hearted in its leap, and it crashed on the rocks, whereas with the MINI, BMW committed. And despite the risks, the MINI had a safer—and more elegant—landing.

The stories of Southwest, Continental, Gatorade, and the MINI Cooper all show a consistent pattern that connects clarity with value. But all these stories were all told from the outside. To be fair, we don't have behind-the-scenes access to the leadership conversations at Continental or at MINI Cooper that would directly link their external performance to internal acts of choice. In the remaining chapters, this will be our goal. We need to open up that black box if we are to see how these fate-making decisions occur. We'll find that, far from being the result of rational analysis, making the leap is often an act of courage.

4

The Shadow Side of Strategy

Most of us operate based on a worldview that business is a rational enterprise. We believe that the essential nature of business can be understood through the analysis of revenues, costs, market share, and other metrics of performance. Executives, according to this worldview, are mostly objective decision-makers. Though their judgment may be clouded or biased from time to time, we assume that the decisions they reach are largely rational.

Based on my experience, I don't believe this is the case. We are better served by flipping our normal way of thinking about things on its head. Rationality is an achievement in business, not the norm.[1] As we saw in the case of Paul, the North American president at Dividio, whose case I introduced in Chapter Two, leaders are often deeply ambivalent about choosing. The dilemma that binds the identity crisis is paralyzing because the risks involved have the power to stir up considerations that have little to do with hard metrics or deliberative judgments about long-term strategy. What appears to observers to be a rational process—which may even feel like one to participants—is really fueled by forces of which we are dimly aware.

The Common App

In 2010, the Common Application was at the threshold of a fateful decision, and it was my job to help lead them through it. Formed in 1975 by a coterie of elite American colleges, the Common Application is a not-for-profit membership association of colleges that in recent years has evolved into the de facto electronic clearinghouse for college applications. The Common Application allows students to complete and submit their college applications to multiple schools using one standard, robust application process. Given its central role in the admissions process, the "Common App," as it is informally known by thousands of anxious high school students and their parents, has become one of the most influential institutions in higher education. Roughly three million applications by 750,000 aspiring college students course through its electronic pipeline. To these applications school guidance counselors, administrators, and teachers submit tens of millions of recommendations, transcripts, and other documentation to support applicants.

The decision that the Common Application's board of directors was about to make would at least double, if not quintuple, those numbers through the decade's end. Throughout 2010, the board had initiated transparent discussions with its community of members—the colleges and universities that accept the Common App—about whether the organization should dramatically expand its footprint in the admissions world.

The Common App had been growing. The organization steadily increased its membership over the years. Of the roughly 1,500 four-year-degree-granting non-profit institutions of higher education in the United States, about 400 were Common App members in 2010. Yet it was still an exclusive group. Owing to the Common App's elite roots, the member institutions were among the most selective in the United States. All had pledged a commitment to "holistic" admissions. In practice, that meant the members agreed to incorporate subjective evaluations of student merit—including essays and recommendations—that went beyond more broad-brush "objective" though scalable assessments like SAT scores, class rank, and grade-point averages. The Common App viewed itself in part as an antidote to the reductionism that characterized the majority of college application systems in the United States. The critical decision the board faced was whether to remove the holistic requirement and open the doors to every eligible college and university in the United States.

Removing the holistic requirement would transform the Common App. The underlying business model would change fundamentally, membership would surge, and the staff would need to grow significantly. Indeed, its very mission was also on the line. From its founding, the Common App's purpose had been a mix of heeding a higher calling and satisfying members' interests. Its core job was to ease the burden of the college application process for students and their parents. Yet as a membership community, the Common App had also pledged to meet the idiosyncratic needs of its selective institutions. And with a board that included the deans of admissions from some of the most selective schools in the country, the Common App retained an elite air. Though membership had grown over the preceding fifteen years, the culture remained intimate and exclusive.

"You're known for the company you keep," admitted one admissions director I asked about the potential expansion. Indeed, many admissions officers of the member schools voiced trepidation over the possibility of growth. "If we grow that fast," said one, "we're saying that the Common App is less special, that it's a commodity." Others felt that removing the holistic requirement would undermine the founding mission.

Others saw the power of getting bigger. A bigger footprint would mean that the Common App could play a more meaningful role in expanding access to higher education for greater numbers of students around the country—particularly disadvantaged students, for whom the Common App would serve as a hub connecting them to a huge array of schools. Because the Common App would maintain a separate membership category for the holistic admissions schools—offering reduced fees as an incentive—many admissions officers believed that growth might further rather than undermine the mission to advance holistic admissions criteria.

After a year's worth of stakeholder engagement and analysis, the board met to make its decision. The choice was far from preordained. I was on hand to guide the board through the process. In advance, my team had prepared a comprehensive analysis of the financials. The board could adjust a number of inputs—much like using dials on a dashboard—to understand the impact of their decisions on membership growth over the course of five years, pricing per application and membership fees, applications per student, applications per institution, revenues, and operating expenses. Understanding the numbers was critical because the Common App's online technology would need a serious upgrade and the board wanted to know whether they could afford it. They also wanted to know whether they could bring down application fees for all member institutions.

The board collegially waded into its final discussion about expansion. I did my part to keep the conversation grounded, helping board members voice their differences, weigh trade-offs, and interpret the implications of what they were wrestling with. But as the conversation unfolded, I was struck by a disturbing thought: I could no longer remember *why* the board considered expansion in the first place. Why drop holistic admission in order to grow? Moreover, I was increasingly concerned that the board had lost touch with that basic question as well. Yes, we had discussed many reasons for expanding *and* for maintaining the status quo. Greater market share would protect the organization from less-exclusive for-profit competitors that had been lurking on the periphery for some time. A larger membership would open up access to under-represented students. The additional revenue would fund a next-generation technology platform that was necessary. But all those reasons had emerged post hoc, thrown in as arguments over the course of the discussion. And now, for the life of me, I couldn't remember why the board had initiated the conversation in the first place. What had been the driving force for this momentous decision?

After the next break, I asked each director to jot down the reason the board had originally posed the question and why it held strategic significance for the Common App. "Why," I asked, "are you considering dropping holistic admission?" I then asked the directors to share what they had written. Their answers were fascinating. Not a single board member could recall the original motive for expansion. Furthermore, each offered a different rationale that implied dissimilar versions of the Common App's core purpose. These differences surprised the group, not because they had divergent feelings about the issue but because they now realized that, in some respects, they had all been having very different conversations.

The board did not perseverate on this observation too long. The directors quickly deliberated and, in a matter of minutes, proposed a new rationale. "We need the operating revenue," they proposed, "to fund the new technology platform."

This conclusion seemed strange to me. Here was a group of smart, thoughtful people. They were painstakingly deliberative. We had just spent six months investigating stakeholder opinion on this issue and debating its merits, and in a matter of minutes a complex set of motivations had been boiled down to a simple question about funding a new technology platform. Perplexed, and feeling drawn onward as if by an invisible force, I felt compelled by the group to move on. But before relenting I thought it wise to circle back to our analysis.

"If that's the case," I said, "let's check the numbers and see if you can fund the upgrade without growing."

Tweaking the dials on our makeshift financial package that I had projected on the screen in front of us, we discovered that the Common Application *could* fund the upgrade without expansion. In fact, they could do so with budget to spare. I looked around at the directors. Shoulders relaxed. People breathed. They seemed relieved. After a short round of comments, we ended the conversation. The Common App decided to retain their holistic admissions policy as it was.

In the 1970s, a group of researchers at Carnegie Mellon University (CMU), led by Nobel Prize–winning economist Herbert Simon, began to test our normal assumptions about rational behavior in organizations. The CMU researchers were fascinated by how organizations made decisions in real life. Did decision making comport with the models that most economists had in their heads? Most people assumed that organizations operated according to some measure of rational analysis. Managers would select a problem or an opportunity that needed attention, identify and debate options for addressing it, and then, based on available information, determine a course of action. But Simon and his colleagues (Michael Cohen, James March, and Johan Olsen) found something entirely different. Decisions were not rational. This was especially true when you put managers together in groups. Teams, the researchers discovered, followed what they dubbed the "garbage-can model" of decision making. In this model, the "garbage can" works less like a rational process than as a collective receptacle into which team members dump a hodgepodge of divergent interests, desires, and problems. From this mélange a "solution" is eventually plucked.

In a 1972 paper, Cohen, March, and Olsen presented a counterintuitive position on group decision making: they argued that the garbage-can model is "a collection of choices looking for problems, issues and feelings looking for . . .

situations in which they might be aired, solutions looking for issues to which they might be the answer, and decision makers looking for work."[2]

I have witnessed hundreds of managerial decisions for which the garbage-can model probably best describes the near-lunacy that can take hold. We tend to believe that senior managers make decisions based on a clear, shared understanding of the problems they face. They factor in well-defined goals and preferences and weigh their options systematically and judiciously. However, my observation is that many managers—especially at the top of the business—can be surprisingly unintentional, even capricious, about the choices they make. Compounding the problem is the fact that the deciders believe that they are operating rationally; they lack self-awareness about the mixture of forces that influence their choices. Thus the decisions they make can be mysterious even to themselves. Many decisions are made almost unthinkingly, as if by default. Moreover, as the Common App story illustrates, the crisscrossing undercurrents that produce these so-called agreements can be remarkably opaque—even to the most thoughtful of us. This leads to a troubling question: If critical decision making in businesses works this way, how can we expect leaders to successfully formulate, choose, and sustain over time the driving purpose of the enterprise?

The Shadow Side of Strategy

To understand the "hidden" nature of the factors that drain logic and rationality from decision making, it's helpful to know where the rational theory of business came from, especially for that quintessential exercise in purpose—the art of making strategy.

In the late 1940s, Bruce Henderson—a Harvard Business School dropout, soon-to-be founder of the Boston Consulting Group, and progenitor of the influential field of strategy—worked for the small-motors division of Westinghouse Electric Corporation. As chronicled by former *Harvard Business Review* editor-in-chief and managing editor of *Fortune* magazine Walter Kiechel in his book *The Lords of Strategy*, his history of the management-consulting field, it was at Westinghouse that Henderson discovered a pattern of behavior that he would see again and again throughout his career, one that would deeply shape his thinking about business.[3]

Henderson learned that Westinghouse was consistently losing money on each gas-pump motor it sold. Why, Henderson wondered, would the company persist in selling a product on which it continually lost money? After investigating further, he concluded that Westinghouse had chosen to distribute a full line of products, including some that lost money, for what he derided as "cultural reasons."

As to what might constitute cultural reasons—or, indeed, whether the company *knew* that it was losing money and continued to sell the products anyway, or was simply doing so unwittingly—we have nothing on the public record. But whatever those reasons might be, Henderson held them in extremely low regard. They contradicted his view of how a company *should* operate: by nurturing and retaining *only* products and lines of business that made money. As he later recalled, "Nearly all companies I have known have a number of businesses they should not be in." The discrepancy between what a company ought to do and what it actually did prompted Henderson to invent diagnostic tools that would eventually lead to the development of the field of strategy.

Grounded in empiricism and equipped with tools built by engineers like Henderson, strategy consultants and academics began to exercise tremendous influence over how executives thought about running a business. However, because their methods and tools weren't built to account for the messy human element, they simply left that part out. If strategy owed a debt to the irrational forces against which it was meant to be a bulwark, the field quickly forgot its taproots. Instead, for the last fifty years strategists have been busily developing ever more sophisticated ways to diagnose and conceptualize the business and its prospects in the market—entirely neglecting the human element. In their calculations, the personal and communal undercurrents of the business, its political and cultural preoccupations, have been seen as mere error variance. Like Henderson, most strategists either dismissed the human element as irrelevant or paid it lip service.

But what if the emotional and cultural economics of the business exert an equal, if not dominant, force in shaping strategy and its execution? What if the so-called hard side of business is softer than we thought?

Kiechel believes that this question has plagued the field of strategy from its inception. In *The Lords of Strategy*, Kiechel offers up a possible subplot to the dominant story of strategy. He appropriates psychologist Carl Jung's idea of a "shadow" to suggest that the passions, fears, anxieties, and desires that constitute the inner workings of a business have been repressed in the interest of advancing technical solutions. But what if we press Kiechel's line of thinking further: What if, rather than being fundamentally an engineering or economic phenomenon, as it is now assumed, business is fundamentally a communal activity? What if, rather than being driven by hard calculations, business is dominated by the ostensibly soft dynamics of culture, politics, and community?

The fight between these two paradigms, hard and soft, has been a central tension in business for decades. Could it be that the tables are finally turning? At a place like Wharton—where I taught executives for a number of years, and which is one of the world's most finance-driven business schools—you are as likely to see an emphasis on people as on conventional business topics like finance, accounting, and strategy. And today, sales of books about the soft side of business easily outstrip those about the hard side. Concepts like emotional intelligence are now common currency in most businesses.

One of the triggers for this soft-side mini-insurgency was a famous and still controversial business book written by two McKinsey consultants: Tom Peters and Robert H. Waterman, Jr. The book was *In Search of Excellence*, and when it was published in 1982 it became a sensation. The authors focused on companies that championed innovative management styles—less hierarchy, more teams, empowered employees *and* customers—ideas that prefigured publications like *Fast Company* and *Wired*. However, at the time that Peters and Waterman were writing their book it was treated within McKinsey as a fringe step-child, far from the hard heart of the firm's core focus on strategy. Perhaps business could become less uptight, but it would always be dominated by reason and numbers.

That viewpoint still holds sway. Although it is true that the soft side has gained legitimacy in many quarters, it remains sequestered from the hard side of business. If you are an executive attending a weeklong Wharton program, you will likely have classes on finance and strategy and also classes on teams and leadership. But they will be taught by different professors, and they won't be treated as in any way connected. Hard and soft may now be equals, but they remain an antagonistic couple.

In this sense, business persists as a divided field. But perhaps it is time for the war between hard and soft to come to an end. If so, purpose is a place for common ground. Hard and soft converge in the act of choosing purpose. Indeed, as we will see next, these two complementary aspects of business are indivisible pieces of the same reality.

The Anatomy of Choice

Before hard and soft can be reconciled, we must first bring the human element out from the shadows.

The sole weakness of the garbage-can theory of decision making is that the model suggests that the various unseen, unacknowledged forces that lead to defective solutions are random or at the very least, irrelevant. The garbage can is like a grab bag: all that matters is what comes out. But that's not really how it works. These forces can be traced back to the hearts and minds of decision-makers as they struggle with the core tensions in the business. The problem is that these forces remain in the shadows, which allows them to remain mysterious as they exert their influence without our knowledge. But suppose they could be seen, acknowledged, and given their due as influential factors?

Ironically, the work of an economist by training—the scholar and strategy guru Michael Porter—gives us the entry point to a unified theory of business.

No one would argue that Porter is a softy. In Kiechel's book, a skeptical academic in the behavioral camp slanders the overly analytic side of strategy by asking, "Where are the people in a Michael Porter strategy?"[4] Indeed, Porter concedes that his theories do little to account for the human element.

"I think it's important to understand that all of my work is positive," he tells Kiechel, "in the sense that it tries to say 'Here's how the world works.' Then the question of how it actually happens, and whether it's conscious or unconscious, and the role various people play in making it happen—that's all really important stuff. But it's not what this work is trying to do." Porter goes on to acknowledge that people's "egos and emotions" are a wild card that sometimes "distorts what actually gets done away from what you might call the economically rational point of view."[5]

It is, of course, my contention that such distortions contribute significantly to the difficulty of choosing. But distortion may not be the real problem. A more pointed argument is that challenges around making big choices about the business are less about the accuracy, consistency, or judgment regarding the facts than the social and emotional dynamics at play. The soft, or irrational, factors aren't about cognitive biases but part and parcel of what it means for humans to make important decisions.

Ironically, it was Porter himself, perhaps more than any other strategist, who anticipated the "soft" side of strategy. Porter declared that strategy was essentially about choice and that choice was inevitably about trade-offs. Moreover, he observed that top leaders tend to find these trade-offs to be deeply "frightening." The reason they are frightening is that the choice arises "when activities are incompatible. . . . When more of one thing necessitates less of another."[6]

Porter would assert that companies like CNN, Continental, Dividio, and countless others struggled because of their leaders' "failure to choose," and that that failure was based in a kind of fear. They could not accept the jeopardy that would ensue when saying yes to one thing also required saying no to another. Porter argued that organizational leaders confuse, blur, or avoid choice in order to minimize the palpable risks and uncertainties of having to decide. This insight—that choice is a frightening experience—is the entry point for integrating hard and soft.

To better understand the central dynamics involved in the act of choice, I need to introduce the work of Larry Hirschhorn, to which this book owes a considerable debt. Hirschhorn is an MIT-trained Ph.D. in economics whose main influences have been, of all things, psychoanalytic. As such, he is the perfect matchmaker for the hard and soft sides of business. Over the course of his career, Hirschhorn became interested in the kinds of questions many people puzzled over but rarely bothered to investigate. Such as: Why do organizations espouse one thing, but do another? What causes a firm to drift from one understanding of the business to another? Why do executives talk so abstractly about their mission?

Hirschhorn noticed that when leaders faced critical choices about the business—particularly choices having to do with the primary task of the organization—they tended to *not choose* in characteristic ways. They hedge their bets, suppress the reality of choice itself, and compromise so as to partially, but never fully, satisfy one concept of the business or another. He discovered that at the root of strategic drift and confusion was the very human capacity for ambivalence. Leaders charged with strategic decision making were unwilling to accept what Hirschhorn called the "primary risk" of choosing one thing over another.[7] Executives are adept at keeping the emotions they experience around choosing in the shadows because they feel that the risks associated with choosing are unmanageable. These risks may be real or imagined, likely or improbable. Whatever their grounding in reality, these risks are often so anxiety-provoking that they are never acknowledged, much less discussed.

For a case in point, let us return to Dividio. Two years had passed between my work with the leadership team—culminating in Paul's departure from the company—and a more recent conversation with Dividio's leaders. In this case, I was on hand not in an open-ended strategy-related role but rather to talk about the importance of leadership, with an emphasis on how leadership is applied to real problems that need solving in the business and addressing them in an honest way. My brief was not to revisit the earlier dilemma concerning which position Dividio should choose. But the matter had remained unresolved, and the passing of time had not diminished the felt sense of urgency to finally crack that nut. So of course the question came up, and I went for it. "All right," I said, "let's talk about what it would take for you all to exercise leadership and solve this problem."

One team member said, "Well, as a leadership team we would embark on a journey to finally create a vision for this organization that really addressed the question." This sounded well-meaning and a first step, but not quite the pivotal action I was looking for.

"Okay," I said. "So you're not *answering* the question, you're *embarking on the journey to do so*. Got it."

They laughed. I then asked them to strip down the choice they faced to its basic elements. In essence, it came down to whether they were willing to create the business of the future even if it meant detracting from the business of today. It was much the same question that Paul had wrestled with two years before.

Instead of trying to jump in with some insight or observation—the consultant's patented way of shaping the development of a solution, and one that I had been guilty of three years earlier—I started asking the group questions that I hoped would bushwhack into the deeper implications of the choice they had framed. I began by asking whether they all agreed that the fear of choosing was the heart of the problem. They looked around at each other and realized they were in agreement. It struck me that, in their expressions and body language, they seemed almost exhilarated to be stepping closer to what felt like dangerous subject matter. This was promising enough to encourage me to push them further.

I often deal with the notion of what constitutes "bad faith" in leadership. I define bad faith as acting in ways that are incongruent with what is really important, what the moment demands. It's when leaders have a sense of what the right thing to do is, but they don't do it. Sometimes bad faith amounts to taking the path of least resistance, even when you know it won't lead to a meaningful solution. So I asked the group to consider the risks of a bad-faith approach to their problem of choosing. They identified two high-risk possibilities, both path-of-least-resistance outcomes:

- **Whiffing:** They would produce an overly vague vision statement, in line with what they'd been doing for the last ten years, which encompassed just enough hot buttons to keep most people happy but still fail to really crack the core dilemma.
- **Flinching:** They would produce a viable migration path to the business of the future, but then cave in when some of the present business's high-value revenue producers screamed bloody murder and refused to buy in.

Then I asked them to spell out what they thought might be the practical consequences of embracing the lead-agency position—which it seemed clear to me they wanted to embrace. Here, the group's imagination was more profuse:

1. Because the transition to become a lead agency would be an explicit move away from specialist work, Dividio would have to try to upsell its client base to a broader set of services.
2. Relatedly, the company would have to cut loose any clients whose interest was *only* in specialist services.

3. Some of the company's valuable revenue producers would either jump ship or be let go, leaving the firm to struggle through a transition period.
4. Because of the nature of Dividio's predominantly specialist present-day business, they would have to admit that they lacked the creative skills needed to be a lead agency.
5. They would have to hire more creative talent.
6. However, much of that newly hired talent would be sitting on its hands for some indefinite period while the firm ramped up its lead-agency accounts and projects.

It was interesting to me that as each of these potential consequences was raised, members of the group spoke about them in ever-softer voices, as though naming the possibilities made the future both more palpable and more dangerous. The change in tone is indicative. A lot of difficulty and turmoil lies between the moment of anticipating a change and choosing to change and the more distant point of achieving the benefits of change. The group was allowing itself to be in touch with the realities of the choice. It's often unpleasant and a little depressing when you stop defending yourself from the implications.

Then I said, "Assuming you do not succumb to bad faith—you embrace the risks and the trade-offs, and you begin to build the future business—when does the moment of truth come?"

Realistically, they saw a continuum of moments of truth. In essence, they said, "It would be when we had to let go of people. We would have to quickly phase out some portion of our specialist business. We would probably hurt our profit and revenue targets for about eighteen months in a significant way."

As Hirschhorn had argued, when stuck between opposing conceptualizations of the enterprise's purpose, leaders often fail to fully acknowledge and accept the *primary risk* of their choice: the potential loss that is required by the inherent trade-offs embedded in the act of choosing. The Dividio group had crossed the chasm and was fully—if also uneasily—engaged with the primary risks of becoming a lead agency.

At that point I said, "You know, if you really believe in this, it's possible everybody here will have to take a 10 percent to 15 percent haircut on your bonus. You won't make your numbers because you'll be phasing out some of the specialist work. At the same time, you'll be investing in new talent. So, would you be willing, for those eighteen months, to take a 15 percent cut knowing that it would prepare you for this future? It's a leap of faith. Would you do it?"

They didn't answer the question. Instead, they all started smiling, as though I had pointed them toward a place they weren't ready to go to that day. It was also a guilty smile, acknowledging that they, too, would have to accept their share of the ultimate consequences and perhaps had not done so in the past.

That ended our workshop. I wasn't there as a strategy consultant. Given my brief, they had gone as far as I could take them. But I could see they had tasted a bit of the future choices they envisioned. It was a step forward.

I had by then been working with Dividio for more than five years, and coming in that day through the leadership door had gotten me further on this question than I had been able to go coming in through the strategy door. This struck me as more than an interesting coincidence.

The Clash of Two Models

A few years ago I consulted to a large academic healthcare system that included three large hospitals connected to a university medical school. For those unfamiliar with academic medicine, it is a messy institution. Because of teaching hospitals' threefold mission to treat, teach, and conduct medical research—each task with its own set of stakeholders, interests, and purposes—they are among the most complex, contentious, and political organizations on the planet. It is as though three mighty rivers meet—each a force in its own right. A recent study noted that academic medicine is like a "perfect storm" for creating conflict and breakdown.[8]

The storm was felt everywhere for Dr. Edward Lawrence, the chief clinical officer of the system—and my client. One of my projects for Dr. Lawrence was to help the system's breast-care clinic, a subunit in the system's larger cancer center. For months, leaders in the system had been banging their heads against the wall about the clinic, which was struggling with even its most basic tasks. Women waited weeks for breast exams. Calls were chronically dropped. In the months preceding our engagement, a number of mammographers had quit, and their positions remained unfilled. Clinic staffers were unhappy. Many would-be patients, discouraged by the long wait to be seen, turned instead to other local hospitals. Solutions had been attempted, but nothing seemed to work. The problems were persistent and pervasive.

The source of the problems was a complex brew of embedded preferences, habits, and status dynamics. The clinic's undergirding organizational arrangements—reporting lines, roles, communication channels, accountability, and decision making—were confusing and unclear, subject to ad hoc manipulation, and now on the verge of breaking down. Everything from buying a microscope to hiring a mammography technician to revising a physician's schedule seemed to kick up dust between the various individuals and groups involved in the decision. It was a quagmire.

And yet, and yet, underneath all that complexity and chaos lay a domineering order. We discovered that all the instances of contentiousness and acrimony could be traced back to a conflict between two different models for how the unit ought to be run. That conflict in turn mirrored a larger contradiction at the heart of the enterprise.

It was Dr. Lawrence who eventually diagnosed the condition. He realized that, even among the organization's executive leadership, there was a surprising disconnect about how to run the organization. It was during a meeting with the top team that he had a stunning epiphany:

"We were talking about 'integrated clinical enterprise' and all the progress we had made over the past few years assimilating the three missions into one system," he said. "And it suddenly struck me that the people in the room were using the same words but actually talking about two totally different models for delivering care. We used the same exact words, but we meant different things! That's when it dawned on me."

I pushed Dr. Lawrence to spell out these divergent models. The first was what he described as "the traditional Hopkins model," after Johns Hopkins University's renowned medical school and hospital system. At Hopkins, the academic departments ran all the clinical care in the system. Clinical training and research were embedded within the professional disciplines—surgery, cardiology, internal medicine, and so on. The second model, arising from healthcare's increasing complexity, wrapped interdisciplinary care around clinical problems. We might call this the "clinical" model. Here specialties come together to treat problems like cancer, epilepsy, trauma, and stroke. The organizing principle is the disease or the illness, not the discipline. The primary unit in this second model was therefore the clinic, service line, or center that treated a particular clinical problem, not the academic department. The logic of the second model was that clinical practice, training, and research should happen in the context of multi-specialty care rather than within the traditional disciplines.

Once Dr. Lawrence had explained the distinctions, I had my own revelation, one that would make an indelible impression on the way I understood organizations thereafter. The undiscussable conflict between the Hopkins and clinical models explained everything we had seen in breast care unit. Each model necessitated a different balance of power between clinical unit and academic department. But because that balance was in dispute at the top (though not discussed), it spilled over into anywhere in the organization where these groups interacted. The acrimony between a mammography technician and a clinic administrator over scheduling wasn't a clash of personalities but instead replicated the touchy relationship between the cancer center director and the chair of the radiology department, which in turn arose from the tension between different ways of conceptualizing how the cancer center ought to be run, which itself stemmed from contradictions in the larger operating model of the entire enterprise. The system was like a fractal in which each part was a miniature version of the whole.

The breast-care clinic illustrated a pattern that we have seen in earlier chapters: no matter where they appear in the organization, many seemingly disparate problems share the same DNA. Confusion at one level means confusion at another.

The question, then, was why hadn't Dr. Lawrence's leadership cohort acknowledged the clash between these two fundamentally different models? There was every opportunity to do so. In a quasi-therapy session with the top twenty-five leaders in the system, we had once asked each to rate how much influence they had on a handful of key strategic decisions. We also asked their opinion of how much influence their colleagues ought to exercise over the making of those same decisions. Once we tallied up the results, the pattern was unmistakable. The dean and the department chairs consistently believed they had more influence over clinical decision making than did their peers on the clinical side. When we asked the group to resolve the discrepancies by clarifying the decision rights on these issues, they found the task incredibly difficult. It was as if they tacitly *preferred* the ambiguity.

Sometime after the consultation, I asked Dr. Lawrence why the senior team couldn't have put the two models on the table and discussed them. "That's an interesting question," he said. "I think there was an element of denial. Rather than recognize that there was this inherent tension—that it was really hard for us to be clear—we pretended it wasn't there. We'd say, 'Oh, everyone understands.' But then everybody would walk out of the room and continue to operate based on their own interpretation of the model."

Dr. Lawrence's observation is critical. The real power of the dilemma that sustains an identity crisis lies in its stealth—the conflict about purpose is often unrecognizable or undiscussable in the day-to-day life of the organization. If you go around asking people about what business the organization is in and how it really runs, you are likely to get some level of surface agreement. But if you look more deeply at the way different people approach important problems, at how the business is structured, at the nature of recurring issues in the organizations—the points of conflict and discomfort—the outlines of the hidden dilemma emerge.

Why do critical choices remain hidden? After all, if organizations acted in purely rational ways, they would be able to surface and address contradictions. This leaves us with the possibility that the core dilemma may be both irrational *and* unconscious. Recall that it took an uncommon stroke of insight—an epiphany—before Dr. Lawrence could recognize the hidden disconnect between operating models about which his colleagues assumed they were in agreement. The identity crisis depends on a hidden contradiction at the very center of the company.

The Family Secret

There are forces—beyond the whims or agendas of even uniquely powerful individuals—that keep such core questions about the business from being publicly discussed. The very persistence of an identity crisis, its destructive impact on the performance of an organization, the emotional undertow people feel when broaching it, and its seemingly covert inner workings all suggest that many of the influential factors affecting the business are hidden from view.

As a partner at Pivot, I count myself guilty of avoiding difficult facts—and of devising ways to cover them up. I have seen and participated as a consultant in remarkably energetic initiatives to keep organizations from confronting the truth. People are amazingly willing to go along with these ploys. The tactics for avoidance vary and can often seem perfectly legitimate. For example, we may reengineer a process, go on a cost-cutting binge, pursue an innovation, create a new marketing scheme, or restructure the business (for the third time in as many years). But such initiatives are often either an ungainly compromise between mutually exclusive philosophies of the business or ways of kicking the unresolved issue down the road. These are defensive strategies for avoiding the possibility of experiencing the risk and loss that accompany big decisions.

Avoiding risk by leaving difficult matters unresolved is a powerful feature of even our most hallowed institutions. *Founding Brothers*, Joseph Ellis's Pulitzer Prize–winning book about the creators of America's experiment in democracy, beautifully illuminates how dilemmas of choice and purpose are managed. Ellis recounts how the early congressional delegates in Philadelphia brokered a number of delicate compromises over slavery and contentious questions about the balance of power between the federal government and the states. The delegates' chief tactic was often avoidance. For example, Congress concluded that rather than residing with the federal government or the individual states, sovereignty rested with "the people." "What that meant," writes Ellis, "was anybody's guess."

Nothing caused greater anxiety than the question of slavery—not only because of the strong differences of opinion among the delegates, but also because slavery exposed the inherent contradictions in the Constitution itself. For some, like Virginia's James Madison, the discussion was so paralyzing that obfuscation became the only possible strategy. Caught between Enlightenment principles on one hand and the planter interests of his home state on the other, Madison refused to be pinned down. Over time, he developed a knack for "artfully contrived ambiguity" to evade the issue.

Madison's cagey behavior wasn't simply an exercise in bad faith. He perceptively believed that the slavery controversy had the potential to destroy the union. Indeed, Ellis argues, the seminal legacy of the revolutionary generation was its successful avoidance of these problems. The founders didn't dare to choose between competing options for what the country should be for fear that they would destroy it. It was, writes Ellis, the "unmentionable family secret." At great human cost, the secret burst into the open when, nearly seventy-five years later, the Civil War began.

The concept of sustaining equilibrium among powerful forces is alluring. It allows you to suppose that choices can be indefinitely postponed. However, my own experiences suggest that balance is a double-edged sword. Yes, it can be used to keep conflict at bay. But at what cost?

The truth is that purpose requires choice, and nearly every significant choice is entangled in trade-offs that must be addressed and risks and loss that must be accepted. That is just the way of things. Efforts to avoid that reality—to avoid the pain and loss of choosing—only postpone or make worse the inevitable day of reckoning.

A Tragic Irony

Like the nascent federation of states, the large academic healthcare system I consulted also had issues of institutional harmony at stake. These issues lay behind the unwillingness of the system's leaders to choose between the two diametrically opposed healthcare delivery models. Dr. Lawrence's epiphany—that an air of superficial agreement helped to hide the underlying discord—led to a further, more disturbing insight: surfacing the conflict would threaten the system's ability to function collegially. Denial, avoidance, and pretense might be awkward to live with, day in and day out, but it allowed the institution to muddle through. Not that the leaders of the healthcare system opted for living a lie, but they had settled for living two uncomfortably incompatible truths. The dysfunction that afflicted the breast-care clinic was but one of the consequences.

Ironically, such entrenched-but-repressed derelictions are fueled by a desire to protect the organization and its people. Dr. Lawrence and the senior team were motivated by a wish to maintain stability and collegiality. To address the advantages of one delivery model over the other would upheave the framework of power and authority by which the leadership team operated—however uneasily. It would spread further anxiety throughout the medical school and in the hospital. Most of all, it would make visible and undeniable the requirement to act. So the team didn't rock the boat. In place of frank discussion, the default strategy was an unsatisfying equilibrium sustained by silence.

As we have seen, avoiding the undiscussable in order to "protect the organization" ends up hurting the organization. "For us to leave this issue unresolved was even riskier than if we had faced it," said Dr. Lawrence. "That's the tragic irony. Being in between was demoralizing for the entire organization." To be sure, as Odysseus understood, making a defining choice always brings trade-offs and loss. But the alternative is worse. Dr. Lawrence was right: being in-between *is* demoralizing. Trying to deny the conflict inevitably sustains it. A senior management team may suppress its tensions temporarily but they will inevitably flare up elsewhere. Left unaddressed, an identity crisis becomes an unending purgatory of needless injuries.

Leaders, consider the high ground here. Confront the choice. And don't expect it to be easy. As Dr. Lawrence and his colleagues began to wade into the contradictions in the organization, things got hot. "The more we push the learning process," one senior executive told me, "the more we uncover and say out loud some of the real glitches in the system. We're bringing to the surface a lot of things that hadn't been said before, and that's getting messy. The stakes are getting higher."

But that's as it should be. The stakes get higher the closer an organization comes to asserting its purpose.

Marrying Hard and Soft

In a 2008 article in the *Journal of Economic Behavior and Organization*, Carnegie Mellon researchers Mie Augier and James

March had something striking to say about the relationship between the *process* by which we make decisions and the actual *experience* of making them. The conventional way of thinking about decisions, they wrote, "emphasizes calculating the relative importance of different values and making a choice that maximizes expected value." Notice here the econometric view of a human being: one who calculates and maximizes. Augier and March found instead that the real world doesn't fit this conveniently rational creature. "In fact, important values forgone are experienced not just as costs," they say, "but also [as] *deep, enduring sorrows and personal failures*" (italics mine).[9] Augier and March aren't talking about quirky cognitive errors that throw off our normally rational calculations. They aren't talking about hindsight bias, the law of sunk investment, or the trap of overconfidence. They aren't talking about errors at all. Rather, they are reminding us—because we need to be reminded—that business is fundamentally about the human condition.

If Michael Porter was reluctant to account for the messy wild card of "egos and emotions," Augier and March sought to enlarge the tent of managerial theory to include the whole human being. This was surely a welcome development. But perhaps it is time to apply this insight more vigorously in the concrete world of business.

I have come to believe that when we marry hard and soft, then fresh insights become available. We see organizational life for what it is, not as strategists, economists, or engineers might like to see it. For example, we see how market shifts put pressure on a company's identity. The greater the degree of change, the more tensions and contradictions arise, making the task of defining the business even more challenging. Inside of companies, we see how big strategy decisions create winners and losers, stirring up strong—though often unacknowledged—feelings of anxiety and loss.

The marriage of hard and soft alters how we see both sides of the equation. One the one hand, the soft opens us up to a broader set of possible explanations for what truly impairs rational strategic decision making. Rather than being a wrong-headed business model or a misreading of the market, perhaps strategy misfires because—as we saw in the case of Dividio—an executive fears betraying close colleagues who would lose if a new path were chosen. In almost every choice, a leader must be able to say no in order to say yes, and—for deep, complicated human reasons—saying no can be profoundly difficult.

On the other hand, insights into hard strategic difficulties can provide us with a more robust way of thinking about so-called soft issues. We see dysfunctions in the business not merely as "people problems" but as upwelling expressions of larger foundational business dilemmas. Thus what may at first appear to be a turf battle between two departments is really descended from a persistent failure to clarify the company's purpose or a painful fight with a coworker is less a personal failure or conflict of styles than evidence of an important strategic dilemma. When hard and soft merge, what once seemed all business begins to feel utterly personal, and what once felt so personal turns out to be scarcely personal at all. Hard and soft interpenetrate.

If hard and soft do come together, we need to think about leadership in new ways. Leadership's primary responsibility is to define the purpose of the business. This means understanding and making choices to resolve strategic dilemmas confronting the organization. Part and parcel of that duty is accepting the reality of trade-offs and the fact that big decisions evoke powerful feelings. An elemental role that leaders play is to wrestle with uncertainty, risk, and the losses caused by doing one thing rather than another.

The executive is therefore anything but a technocrat. His or her work is deeply psychological. The executive's decisions and commitments are (and ought to be) visceral, infused with feeling. If they are not, than something is going wrong. Indeed, the executive ought to view him- or herself as an instrument for identifying such feelings. One of the most striking symptoms of an enterprise in an identity crisis is the gut-level unease executives often have about what is happening within them. A top team may feel stuck, but they lack the vocabulary to describe the dilemmas that underlie the crisis. "Maybe the problem is *me*" was all that Paul could muster to express his consternation over Dividio's dilemma.

But symptoms can be identified and a vocabulary developed to describe them. Leaders can learn to spot the signs of an emergent dilemma. When uncomfortable conflicts and contradictions appear in the business, we all know that people find ways to speak of them in code. They talk around the edges of big issues without acknowledging them directly. An incipient identity crisis becomes, like a family secret, elusive and—seemingly by unspoken agreement—undiscussable. Yet, as we've learned, the crisis can be identified the discomfort it causes.

What this means for executives is that you can often gain more insight about what's wrong with your company's strategy by searching your feelings about the business, and those of the people around you, than by simply looking at the numbers (or by doing the reverse and using the reality of numbers to surface highly undiscussable feelings about the business). In either case, you may discover that what people say about the business doesn't match with what the business is actually doing, or as with Dr. Lawrence, that the supposed agreements mask real differences in how things are and should be. You may get an uneasy feeling—which you don't want to share with others or even admit to yourself—that there is a kind of duplicity spreading through the business.

Paradoxically, the shadow side of strategy calls out for a more muscular approach to the soft stuff and a more attuned approach for the hard. If you are a leader and you sense there is an issue that seems to lie outside the bounds of rigorous, rational debate, take that as a clue. Recognize that something is happening. Think about why it may be difficult to address. What are the differences in views on this subject? Why can't they be discussed? What's the uncomfortable truth from which people are running away?

Frightening as they may be, the big purpose-defining choices in business are moments for leaders to rise to greatness—in part because the choices are so difficult, but also because the stakes are worthy of the emotions they provoke. Consequently, wrestling with fate-making choices shouldn't be seen as unmitigated doom and gloom. When the clarifying moment is finally seized, and a defining commitment is made, I have seen that executives sometimes experience genuine exhilaration—the life-affirming courage one feels when making a leap of faith.

"Faith," "feeling," and "courage" are not words we normally use when talking about business. But in my experience there are few things executives find as satisfying and leaderly as creating clarity and coherence in the business or of taking a risk with their colleagues to do the right thing. In the next chapter we'll see exactly how this happens.

5

Taking a Stand

Karen Zorn's family believed in being true to one's principles. "My father was an elected official in my home town in Wisconsin," Zorn told me as we recounted her journey over the last two years. "He was the kind of guy who took risks and didn't care what people thought. He probably shouldn't have been elected twice. But he had grit. He was the same at home as he was in public. I learned very early on that there was something more important to him than being liked. My father taught me that it is more important to do the right thing."

Zorn and I talked often, and at length, about her strategy as president of the Longy School of Music, a nearly-hundred-year-old institution in Cambridge, Massachusetts. We had met three years earlier, in 2009, when Zorn asked me to help her through an ambitious effort to turn the school's fortunes around. Off and on for the ensuing year, I rode shotgun at Zorn's side—along with her senior staff and Longy's board of trustees—for what often felt like a roller coaster of uncertainty, providence, and exhilaration. From my vantage point as consultant, I could see now how Zorn had put her father's principles into action. She had taken an unpopular stand that enabled the venerable institution to overcome an Odyssean dilemma and restore the school's clarity of purpose.

Back in 2009 there were plenty of difficult tests at Longy, but two stood out.

First, Longy was losing money. Recent financial projections suggested that the school could run for maybe one more academic year before it collapsed financially. The recession had hit Longy hard. Charitable donations were down. But the real cause of the crisis was expenses. Before Zorn's arrival, Longy's board and its former president concluded that faculty members were underpaid. To remedy the situation, they instituted faculty raises as high as 18 percent that would accrue over the following three years. The board assumed that the raise could be paid for through fundraising—but that was before the Great Recession.

Second, like many of the organizations we have examined in previous chapters, Longy was an institution at odds with itself. Although the school had begun to articulate a new vision under Zorn's leadership, there were powerful, long-standing contradictions in Longy's identity that had sown inefficiency, compromise, and conflict throughout its various activities.

Primary among these was whether Longy's mission was to prepare students for elite performance. Was Longy, like Juilliard and other big-name conservatories, a place where students came to train for coveted jobs in major orchestras, symphonies, and other venues? Or was Longy training students for careers beyond elite performance—to be, for example, music teachers, studio performers, or people using their classical training as a vehicle for community engagement? These aren't just two different missions; they represent two very different strategic positions that cater to two very different classes of customers.

I remember feeling the dissonance the first time I sat down with Zorn. She and her team shared with me a rough draft of Longy's first strategy plan, and I thought how ambiguous their positioning had been on this question. The plan had that cagey "motherhood and apple pie" kind of feeling that I had seen in other strategic plans that masked the ambivalence of their authors. Perplexed, I asked her, "Well, which is it? Are you guys competing head-to-head with the Juilliards of the world, or not?"

She replied with silence.

Conservatory Roots, Contemporary Reality

In 1915, Georges Longy, then the eminent principal oboist of the Boston Symphony Orchestra, founded Longy to provide comprehensive training in musicianship and performance, in emulation of the French conservatory model. In the course of its illustrious history, Longy School has counted many first-rank musicians among its graduates. It has also, over the years, attracted an equally distinguished faculty of luminous performers.

The historic mission of the school was to train elite composers and performers. Increasingly, however, Longy attracted fewer musicians with elite potential than did the likes of Juilliard, Boston's New England Conservatory, or Philadelphia's Curtis Institute. At the same time, the school had been quietly earning a strong reputation for producing talented teachers of music and for its programs of community outreach and engagement. However, those activities tended to be seen as lower-status ventures.

"In the music world," says Zorn, "the highest status is to make your life as a performer or a conductor. Then comes conservatory teacher. Even as a conservatory teacher, you're still performing. But if you teach in a public school, people think you aren't a performer." Consequently, in the performance-based pecking order, public-school teachers and similar educational roles are relatively second-class. (Interestingly, Zorn told me that outside the small circle of elite stars the annual incomes for performing musicians and public school music teachers are far more equal than their relative status would suggest.)

Status, however, didn't align with the needs of the market for musicians. The demand for music teachers was greater than the demand for performers. And the number of sought-after roles in performance were limited. Being the first violin at the Boston Symphony Orchestra is like playing for the Celtics—very, very few can make it. Moreover, demand for advanced music education remained consistently high because so many people aspire to elite performance. Thus the infrastructure for producing elite talent far exceeded the number of career opportunities available in performance while also failing to meet the much larger demand for careers beyond performance. The market had hitherto failed to deliver a solution to this problem. The simple fact was that conservatories catered to a very small subset of students.

This is a growing disconnect that many schools of music are not eager to acknowledge—even to themselves. Only a

small percentage of music students rise into the elite performing ranks. Schools therefore need to help their students be
open-minded about pursuing other rewarding options. Increasingly, that has meant offering programs geared to music teaching and to engaging local communities to embrace the value
of music participation and appreciation. Some schools—
inspired by both a passion for music and the goal of growing
the overall market—had begun to broaden and democratize
access to music instruction. Longy had become one of the
leaders in this area but had done so ambivalently. Longy was
unwilling to sacrifice the status associated with training elite
performers, even though it was clear that the school was no
longer competing with the top echelon of elite-performance
conservatories.

A colorful old baseball cliché says that the mission of every
batter is to "hit it where they ain't." Zorn, a classically trained
pianist-turned-administrator, had natural instincts for this
kind of thinking. Longy was Zorn's first top job, but she had
developed a keen sense for market segmentation before assuming the role. As a senior administrator and faculty member at
Boston's Berklee College of Music, Zorn had seen how Berklee
planted its flag in the world of contemporary music, becoming
one of the first institutions to offer elite instruction outside
the classical genre. Berklee's mission statement describes the
school as "the world's premier learning lab for the music of
today—and tomorrow."

Zorn was naturally attracted to Longy by the idea—already
enunciated by the board of trustees and the previous president—
that the school must become more in tune with the realities
of how most classically trained musicians actually make a

living, helping students learn to be entrepreneurial in building their careers in music, going even beyond the bounds of orchestral performance in large markets. But although the school had voiced its intention to go beyond performance, it hadn't made the commitment.

I should mention that this kind of equivocal, hesitant commitment is quite common in business. It occurs when an organization feels pressure to transition to new realities but is not yet willing to accept the consequences of deciding to do so. You've heard the expression "crossing the Rubicon"—meaning passing a point of no return? This kind of fateful decision happens in strategy too. It is often not the first but the second encounter with a pivotal choice—at its point of no return—that creates the moment of truth for an organization.

Facing the Facts

In the spring of 2009, Zorn pushed to create a new plan for Longy that would turn around the business and reposition the school. At the beginning of this process, we pulled together a small group consisting of Zorn; members of her senior team; Bonny Boatman, then the board chair; and, over time, a varying constellation of other board members. On the agenda were a number of existential questions: whether to consider being acquired (Cambridge neighbor Lesley University was a possible suitor), whether Longy could or should execute a turnaround on its own, and how best to adapt the school's identity so that it could thrive in a changing music marketplace.

The first task was to take an honest and unflinching look in the mirror. Preparing to make a choice often begins with establishing a deep, shared understanding of the business. Therefore, the team began with the numbers. They analyzed three revenue streams—undergraduate, graduate, and community programs. None was performing particularly well, but the graduate school (the conservatory) produced more revenue than the two other sources. And community programs had been steadily losing money or contributing relatively little to the bottom line.

A hard look at the numbers enabled the team to begin unwrapping the essence of Longy's strategic challenge, which for a long time had remained hidden from view. The financial findings were relatively straightforward. Much more complicated was interpreting what lay behind them. The numbers were a necessary start. Paradoxically, it is often the impersonality of the numbers that leads toward undiscussable subjects that would otherwise be too political, personal, or emotionally charged to broach.

One such undiscussable was the question of why Longy would persist in an unprofitable business that put its survival at risk. You may recall it was just this question that eventual Boston Consulting Group (BCG) impresario Bruce Henderson raised but then dismissively dropped during his tenure at Westinghouse. He was less interested in *why* someone would invest in a business that lost money than *how* to fix it. But by dismissing so-called "cultural" issues, had Henderson missed something crucial?

Longy's story shows us the value of digging deeper. Seemingly inconsistent or contradictory behaviors are far more than mere glitches in the system to be fixed; they reveal a lot about the inner workings of the business. For example, despite the varied financial performance of its revenue centers, Longy historically had treated all three as being equal in value. We might wave off this stance as evidence of normal non-profit egalitarianism. But this would be a mistake. Contrary to the stereotype, non-profits care about money. More important, when any organization—whether it is a non-profit or, as we'll see in the next chapter, a Wall Street bank—treats its lines of business, without reflection, as equal to one another, that should raise a red flag that a choice is going unaddressed.

Remember, choice is inherently discriminating. Choice focuses. It prioritizes. It weighs. It establishes some things as more valuable or strategically crucial than others. Yet in business, to publicly declare one thing more important than another can feel like an act of violence. We instinctively avoid decisions because we don't want to injure people associated with less valuable activities or lose our own connections to things we care about. This taboo is so strong that one of my clients called the act of cutting resources to underperforming or nonstrategic projects "drowning your puppies." Disturbing as that image was, the dark humor of this phrase enabled the organization to have more-direct conversations about what mattered while still acknowledging the pain of "killing off" something that you love. It is not coincidental that the word "decide" derives from the Latin word *decider*, which means "to cut off" or "to kill."

Questioning the equality of the three programs or the role of community programming at the school was certainly taboo at Longy. "Even asking questions," says Zorn, "would start people worrying that 'Karen is going to get rid of the community programs.'" Nonetheless, it was appropriate to ask *why* community programs were so critical to the school. The answer to *this* question would bring us one step closer to the core of Longy's crisis.

Why support an underperforming line of business? Ostensibly, community programs existed in order to serve the community. That by itself might have provided a sufficient base of motivation, but certainly not enough to jeopardize the financial sustainability of the school. The financial analysis showed that private lessons and many of the community classes were barely or not at all profitable. Likewise, educational music programs offered in the community—often built around the enthusiasms of particular faculty members—were frequently undersubscribed and sometimes cancelled. Longy assumed that the school's proximity to Harvard Square meant that the community would have a natural appetite even for highly esoteric programming. But the numbers had so far not borne that out. Despite losing money, the programs were allowed to continue.

If many community programs weren't in demand by the community, why then did they continue? Two questions can open things up for an organization faced with apparently contradictory behaviors. The first question is about interests: Whose interests were the community programs serving? The second question is about risk: What risk would Longy (or its leaders) face if community programs were cut? What was Longy afraid to lose?

If we apply these questions to Longy, we end up with a complex political and strategic dilemma. Beyond meeting the needs of would-be customers, community programs had evolved over time to meet the interests of faculty members and (to a lesser extent) the board of trustees. Eliminating or significantly altering the status quo would have meant upsetting these two powerful groups. To understand how this might play out, we have to understand how things worked at Longy.

Longy faculty earned wages in one of two ways: for teaching degree students in the conservatory or for teaching a wide range of non-degree students (children, music aficionados, and amateur performers) from Cambridge and the surrounding area in the community programs division of the school. Many of the students from the adult community programs were or became charitable donors to the school, and many of the most involved and most generous donors were appointed to the board of trustees. The board and faculty were thus linked through community programming. One might argue that this was a good thing. Perhaps charitable donors compensated for the high costs of community programming. Unfortunately, that logic had become increasingly tenuous. Giving had in fact declined. Community programs had therefore become, in effect, a labor market for faculty and a source of culture and connection for members of the board. They were also a large cost for the school.

In reality, community programming met needs that stood apart from the interests of Longy as an institution. The natural affinity that developed between board members and their instructors explained the programs' persistence—as well as why mounting any challenge to their status might have proven difficult.

This hypothesis sheds light on other incongruent facts. For example, Longy had 170 faculty members on payroll in 2009, a considerable number for a school of Longy's size. Faculty were also free to teach at competing schools, which many did. In hindsight, we can see why the board agreed to such high raises for faculty, even when the revenues to support it could not be accounted for. I would stress that the board and the faculty were not coconspirators in having deliberately sought these kinds of outcomes. In my experience such convoluted arrangements are implicit. They accrue unintentionally over time. Longy faculty and board members were simply people, united in their love of music, who had built affinity through the traditional model of musical instruction and apprenticeship. There are no bad guys here, just conflicting interests.

We can make a number of inferences from these observations. First, by virtue of instructors' close connections to many board members, the faculty had acquired a share of institutional power that destabilized the school. Second, the community programs had been designed to serve purposes *other than* meeting the financial needs of the school or serving the broader mission of the conservatory, which was to train degree students. Third, at a deeper level, a closer look at community programming shows us that Longy was conflicted about its core purpose. This conflict wasn't *just* about whether the school trained elite performers or prepared musicians to be teachers. The tension was also about which constituency Longy served. Was Longy a platform designed primarily to meet the diverse needs of the community (faculty included) or to serve the students that enrolled in its conservatory? After the first round of planning, Zorn began to feel that beneath all the entangled and complex issues at Longy there were foundational questions to answer.

The Gordian Knot

The Gordian knot is said to have adorned an oxcart in the central square of Phrygia in what is now western Turkey. King Midas (he of the golden touch) offered the oxcart to the god Zeus as an expression of gratitude after Midas's father, Gordius, was named king. The knot was an intricately woven mystery, beautiful yet intractable—insoluble by human hands. For several hundred years, the knot remained unloosened.

Then, in 333 BC, its mystery tempted Alexander the Great. The young Macedonian's army was camped in Phrygia for the winter. Alexander had heard tales of the knot and couldn't help but visit the puzzle that had eluded so many for so long. Naturally, a great crowd came to watch as Alexander knelt beside the knot and searched for the ends. But, like others before him, he failed to find the solution.

Befuddled, Alexander closed his eyes and sat for some time, searching his mind for an answer. Then suddenly insight struck him. He quickly stood, raised his sword, and with a swift strike cleaved the knot in two. Thereupon, the riddle of the Gordian knot was revealed: hidden inside its core were the two ends.

The Gordian knot is an apt metaphor for an identity crisis that occurs when organizations lose purpose. The condition is bound up in an intractable, knotty network of problems, the sources of which we can't readily identify and may not easily comprehend. There are hidden interests at play, and layers of politics. Most crises last for years. CNN, for example, has suffered from its identity crisis for nearly a decade. Even a company like Dividio, on the leading edge of technological change, can struggle for years. The same may have been true at Longy. When I suggested to Bonny Boatman, the chair of Longy's board, that their strategy seemed to be a concession between two different ideas of what the school wanted to be, she replied with a wry smile and an observation of her own, "Longy has been compromising for a hundred years."

So what does this leave us with? I would argue that the crisis, like the Gordian knot, cannot be solved by solving a multitude of puzzles one strand at a time. The humbling truth is that the knot is often beyond the powers of even the greatest leader. And the painstaking, bit-by-bit approach to executing strategic change simply takes too long. And before you know it—like the allegorical "boiling frog"—you've been cooked to death by degrees. Sadly, many organizations do not notice what's happened until it's too late.

But do not abandon hope! There is a solution. Like Alexander, we can cut directly through to the heart of the matter. But to do this we have to begin with purpose.

Longy and the "Musician of the 21st Century"

I want you to think of purpose as the opposite of the murky middle. Let's be honest: though it may be painful, it is relatively easy to muddle along in the murky middle. You can follow the path of least resistance. You can avoid discussing the undiscussable trade-offs. You can satisfy everyone's interests, not completely but enough to keep up a fairly balanced equilibrium. As CNN has shown, balance can be sustained for quite some time. But what if CNN were to finally break the ice and have an open conversation about its future? Imagine if the network's executives set the options for what it might become side by side and actually *felt* the scary-but-exhilarating implications of each identity. They'd get beyond tactics and abstract ideas and finally plunge into the visceral experience of what the transition to a changed identity would look and feel like. Dividio got a taste of this—just enough to open the door and feel the buzz of what might lie on the other side. Longy, as we'll see, went right on through. To understand how, you have to understand the process of how they got there.

The greatest weapon against the murky middle is to rigorously envision what it would mean to enact a new identity—that is, what it would mean to make the choice. Warning: this process should be slightly traumatizing. If there aren't elements in an unfolding scenario that distress you or make the hairs stand up on the back of your neck, then you haven't done your job. The litmus test for a meaningful purpose ought to be that the vision of the future is both exhilarating *and* scary.

The process has two parts. First, you and your team must build a holistic understanding of what the business would be like if you went all in. Don't pull any punches. In fact, when in doubt, sharpen the blade. If you think a line of business might be a misfit in the new world, imagine you will have to cut it off. Don't shy away from the would-be purpose; embrace it. Second, you have to help the community of your organization get in touch with the implications of a potential future so that they, too, can understand what feels right and what doesn't.

Remember, the anxieties that feed the crisis don't come from an uncertainty about whether you get the math right (the math matters, but that's not what generates the crisis). The anxieties derive from the implications of the choice itself: the economic, social, political, and ultimately the emotional trade-offs of doing one thing versus another.

As a matter of practice, the outlines of your purpose ought to remain clear and clean. As a small illustration, consider PayPal—about which we will hear in more detail in the next chapter. The payments company put together one of the boldest statements of a new purpose and identity I have yet seen. In fact, they laid out two alternatives. The first purpose was to more or less maintain the status quo: enhance its utility role as an online platform for payments, primarily for its parent company eBay. The second purpose was far more audacious. It involved reimagining the way consumers and companies use money, envisioning itself in historical terms as altering the foundations of commerce. PayPal would go beyond the online space and into the offline space to enable people to pay and be paid anytime, anywhere, in any way they chose. This dramatic choice would require monumental changes for the business. Instead of competing solely as an online payment provider, PayPal would go offline and enter the physical world to become a payment vehicle of choice more broadly. They would issue a digital wallet, bet big on mobile technologies, and move from focusing mostly on merchants to serving consumers.

To clarify the distinctions between options A and B, the senior team spelled out the presumed implications of this fate-making choice in a three-page document. In sharp, clear English, they cut straight to the heart of the choice and left no room for a murky middle. This was a blunt confrontation with choice.

Longy would define its new purpose with similar rigor. Although senior management did the numbers and the board analyzed a possible merger with Lesley University, Zorn thought more deeply about Longy's role in the world of music. *What was Longy's problem to solve?* Remember, purpose isn't about a specific product or service; it's about the calling your company answers in the market. It's about righting a wrong in the world.

Zorn realized a wrong that needed righting in the music world. Students who fell short of the elite ideal, of whom there were many, were left unprepared to pursue meaningful alternatives. Moreover, elite performance was a relatively small portion of the market compared to the realistic options for how a classically trained musician could make a livelihood. This was a big problem for which there was no adequate solution. Though Zorn wouldn't have put it this way, the essence of the problem Longy sought to solve in the market was to transform a traditional Plan B, which had been a consolation prize, into a first-class calling.

There were of course nuances to this problem-to-solve. Zorn recognized that a pedagogical limitation of training elite performers was that students seldom attained enough self-awareness about *how* they did what they did. Performers didn't have the training to be teachers. "Performers make better teachers when they're *trained* to be teachers," says Zorn. She also found the reverse to be true: The best teachers know how to perform. It isn't simply a matter of mastering music theory or texts. "You teach from the depth of your own understanding," she told me.

Zorn believed that this might be the purpose for Longy to embrace. The school was well positioned to develop strong music teachers and, moving beyond that, to strengthen programs that would train students to use music to make a difference in the world. Distinguishing itself from the exclusive conservatories that trained a small number of elite performers, Longy would instead expand the horizons for what constituted a classically trained music career. Zorn and her team began to call their vision the "Musician of the 21st Century."

The idea behind the Musician of the 21st Century was to not only train students to be performers but also allow them to cultivate a life in music whose dimensions went well beyond the confines of the main stage at Lincoln Center or Carnegie Hall. Methodologically, what she had in mind was something akin to the way a teaching hospital trained medical residents through the deep, intense experience of performing medicine. In addition to performing, students would learn to teach in public schools and private studios, to learn composing, arranging, production, and the business skills required to build and sustain careers in music.

The Musician of the 21st Century concept would mean redefining Longy's identity. Zorn's plan flipped the priorities at the school. Where performance had long been king, it would now serve a greater purpose. Students had traditionally come to Longy to become elite performers. Learning to teach, educate, or influence communities was secondary to the main goal of performance. Now training students to engage their communities through performance and teaching would be Longy's primary purpose. Instead of being merely an option to fall back on if things didn't work out, teaching would be a means—as vital and as valid as performance—through which students could make a difference.

Having carved out an alternative vision of the school, Longy, like PayPal, now faced the classic Scylla-or-Charybdis choice (related in Chapter Two). Would they be willing to embrace this new purpose wholeheartedly? As Zorn put it at the time, "If we don't change, we will slowly die. But if we change the way we need to, it will radically transform who we are. And some will lose."

So what would the Musician of the 21st Century really look like? How would Longy have to change? What would be gained? What would be lost? Remarkably, the material implications for the organization emerged over the course of one intense meeting that included Zorn, members of her senior management team, and myself. As a design principle, we posed a simple question: What would Longy look like if we were to completely rebuild it around the Musician of the 21st Century concept? Naturally, the final product was a bit messy and incomplete—no strategy pops forth fully formed, like Athena from Zeus's brow. But the prototype design that the group produced would have enough punch to lead to an inflection point in the business.

The projected new Longy had several critical features. First, the school would have to align each of its programs to serve the goal of training students to become great music ambassadors—whether as performers, music teachers, or educators engaging the community. The group proposed strengthening and aligning activities at the school that would enable Longy's purpose and cutting those that wouldn't. The first difficult insight from this process was that the school had spread itself too thin. It would have to focus. If Longy was to pursue its purpose, the heart of the institution would have to be the conservatory. That was where they trained graduate-level musicians near the beginning of their careers. It was also the school's main revenue engine. The decision to accentuate the graduate program led inexorably to a far more difficult question for the team. If the undergraduate and community programs didn't support the conservatory, should they be eliminated?

The group quickly realized that undergraduate education, when compared to the graduate program, didn't support the school's new purpose. In keeping with the principle we had set out at the beginning of the discussion, which was to build out a strategy that fully embraced the 21st Century Musician concept, the group decided to phase out the program over the course of four years. (As of this writing, this decision has since been revisited. Although undergrads account for less than a quarter of Longy's full-time enrollment of 215 students, developments since that time have suggested a place for undergraduate education in the idea of the 21st Century Musician.)

The issue of the community programs, however, was less clear-cut. Indeed, when properly understood, they had the potential to be strategically valuable to the new mission. Although they sapped precious resources, they offered Longy the perfect vehicle for training graduate students. The problem was that, by and large, graduate students weren't teaching in the community programs; only faculty members were. Zorn and her team realized that they had to tie graduate conservatory and community programs together so that each reinforced the other. Currently, the two were motivated by different interests and operated more or less independently. Community programs—consisting of non-degree instruction for children and adults, tutoring, and music enrichment classes—had developed in an ad hoc way and for purposes orthogonal to Longy's emerging mission.

To resolve the mismatch between conservatory and community programs, Zorn suggested a seemingly subtle but meaningful shift. Going forward, community programs would be critical only to the extent that they served as a vehicle for graduate students to learn, experientially, how to teach and how to interact with a community. Thus they would exist *in the service of* the conservatory. Up to this point, the situation had been almost the reverse, with the conservatory providing the financial resources for supporting the community programs. Longy's new system would reorder not only the logic of key activities in the business but also the motivating forces that governed them.

Thus Zorn and her team proposed beefing up weak spots, cutting activities and resources, and realigning the logic of the organization. Other changes quickly came into focus:

○ Longy needed a core group of faculty members who were 100 percent dedicated to the more coherent educational mission Zorn was proposing. Therefore, Longy would deepen its own commitment to those faculty members who devoted a significant amount of their teaching to Longy, rather than to competing institutions.

◦ The faculty needed to be deployed more strategically. For example, if Longy sought to grow the number of candidates for its graduate programs, faculty members could promote the Longy brand by teaching master classes on college campuses around the country.

◦ In order to accomplish Longy's transformation, the team estimated that perhaps as many as one-third of all faculty positions, all part-time, would have to be eliminated.

◦ Finally, the team agreed that Longy would need to admit, unashamedly, that it was no longer going toe-to-toe with the Juilliards of the world. This notion had become more than an expensive pretense; it had also prolonged the school's stay in the murky middle. If they believed in the changes they were advocating, they would have to embrace them wholeheartedly.

Interestingly, the more clearly the strategy came into focus, the easier it was to identify activities, resources, and priorities that clashed with Longy's new purpose. They stuck out like a sore thumb. As we pruned the now-unnecessary elements, the business-to-be came together as a coherent whole. There was a feeling in the room that something elegant was emerging. "If we do this right, we have a real story to tell," said Zorn. "We could even be ready for a major fundraising push for the [Longy] centennial."

By the session's end, the group had drawn a simple schematic showing the main features of the new strategy and how they would restore the school's financial and mission-related vitality. The group felt that what they'd said "no" to was just as important as what they'd affirmed. The schematic therefore showed, in bright red, the assets and program elements that would be cut. Zorn, it would seem, was sailing in the direction of Scylla.

Debunking Old Myths

On a Saturday four weeks later, at the Sheraton Commander Hotel in Cambridge, Zorn and her leadership team presented the new strategy to Longy's full board of trustees. Zorn got straight to the point. The school, she said, was at a "pivotal moment in its history." Then, to clear the air for what was to follow, she proceeded to inventory the "myths" upon which Longy had long been operating:

- There is a belief that all of the school's programs should be treated as equals, that Longy is a democracy, and that *that* is what makes it special.
- Because Longy is special, it is self-evident to prospective students why they should enroll.
- The school must tailor its programs to meet the faculty's needs.
- It is the job of the school to recruit students for the faculty rather than enlist the faculty to recruit students to the school.
- Everyone knows that community programs are the school's bread and butter—they are what makes the place run.
- Longy competes head-to-head with prestigious programs such as Juilliard, New England Conservatory, and Curtis Institute.

One by one, based on her team's analysis and discussion, Zorn knocked the myths down. The board members sat silent, apparently stunned. (When I talked with her recently, I asked

Zorn what she had been thinking when she cut to the chase so bluntly. She replied that the urgency of adopting the new strategy "had to be absolutely clear. I had been too polite and mealy-mouthed with the old strategy.") Rather than underplay the differences between the old strategy and her new proposal, Zorn leaned into them. It was, in a sense, like plowing under the old crop before planting the new one.

Notice the pattern we have established thus far in the book. If there is common ground among MINI Cooper's BMW, PayPal, and Longy, it is that they had sharpened rather than suppressed the differences between their identity and that of others.

After laying out the new strategy, Zorn did not immediately ask for the board's response. Instead, she suggested that the members break out into four groups for more granular round-robin briefings with members of her senior team. This allowed board members to push back on specifics and see how the strategy's parts aligned with the whole. It was also an opportunity for Zorn and others on the senior team to show off the substantive depth of their thinking and the extent of their enthusiasm and unanimity.

"We set the tone," Zorn says of that meeting, "and each of us on the senior team did our part." Together, they laid out the numbers and their implications, the vision for the future, and what it would take to achieve it.

Zorn's bold opening salvo had been a necessary leap of faith. She'd had no idea in advance how the board would receive it. And she was going against the grain of the board's congenial relationship with the faculty, which would, at the very least, make the hill that much steeper to climb. But Zorn believed in the rightness of the plan. She had assumed a heavy responsibility for redefining Longy's business. And the senior team had her back.

If anything, the leap had created clarity. Think back to Chapter One and the glitzy grand ballroom rollout of a "new" strategy that turned out to be so much less than met the eye. This was its antithesis: bold, significant, fully formed, difficult to execute, and a direct challenge to the status quo.

When the Longy board reconvened after the small-group briefings, its members stood one by one and made comments. In my consulting role, I reminded the board that the plan embodied difficult trade-offs. The faculty would be reorganized, the curriculum would change, new priorities would be established, and programs would be restructured and aligned. I noted that it was nearly inevitable that these changes would lead to efforts on the part of some stakeholders to influence the board.

After a series of comments, a venerable and long-standing board member named stood up and, with unmistakable conviction, declared, "We must give Karen our trust."

That did it. By the end of the afternoon the board had approved the strategy.

And thus began the transformation at Longy. The old strategy had been a muddle, just as it was at CNN. Phil Griffin, the president of MSNBC, had once said of his network's rival, "We stand for something and CNN doesn't. . . . [T]hat's their biggest challenge." Like CNN or Dividio, Longy had been stuck in the murky middle. It had failed to make a defining commitment about the business. But here Zorn, her colleagues, and the school's board of trustees had taken a stand.

Getting buy-in from the board was an enormous boost for Longy's new strategy. But getting it proved to be only one of a number of further tests the school's leadership would face. As we'll see, there is a considerable gap between knowing the right thing to do and being able to turn the organization's full energy toward executing it. Choice must give way to action. We must now look at the stakes for a leader who makes a firm commitment to one identity over another.

Gaining by Giving Up

To take a stand, the leader must face the anxiety of making a choice whose ramifications directly affect people. As we have seen, anxiety can quickly deplete the will to take action. Think of poor Hamlet, Shakespeare's embodiment of conflicted indecision, who moaned that "the native hue of resolution is sicklied o'er with the pale cast of thought." Hamlet is saying that overthinking things sometimes gets in the way of mobilizing the natural energies that resolution requires.

Choice can be agonizing, not just because one risks choosing wrongly, but also because the act of making a commitment is emotional, political, and often deeply personal work. To give you a sense of this, let's return to 1984 and briefly consider the early history of another successful technology innovator just down the road from Apple. The company is Intel Corp. And we are in Santa Clara, California, where founders Andy Grove and Gordon Moore felt pressure to make a defining commitment of their own.

Intel's early success had come from manufacturing computer memory chips, known as DRAM (for dynamic random access memory). By 1983, Intel faced growing competition from Japanese manufacturers, which had flooded the market with cheap, high-quality DRAM alternatives. At the time, Intel was entirely identified with the memory business. "The company had a couple of beliefs that were as strong as religious dogmas," observed Andy Grove. One of these was that memory chips "are the backbone of our manufacturing and sales activities."[1]

Way back in 1971, Intel had designed the first commercial microprocessor—essentially, the brain of a microcomputer (later known as the personal computer)—and by 1983 both Grove and Moore saw an opportunity for Intel to move the business toward microprocessor manufacturing. There were even scientists in Intel's R&D group who were eager to make the jump. But the leaders hesitated, unwilling to jeopardize the memory business, which still provided the bulk of Intel's revenues.

It was a classic dilemma, and as the years rolled on, indecision cost the company. By the early 1980s, declining DRAM profits were materially hurting Intel. On what would later be known as Black Monday, fifteen Intel engineers who had been busy designing new microprocessor applications resigned in protest over the company's evident reluctance to seriously commit to the new technology. Intel was riven with disagreement. The proposal to exit the DRAM business ran up against powerful emotions throughout the organization. "It was a grim and frustrating year," Grove later recalled. "We had lost our bearings. We were wandering in the valley of death."

One day in the middle of that bad year, as Moore and Grove stared glumly out of Grove's office window, Grove turned to Moore and asked, "If we got kicked out, and the board brought in a new CEO, what do you think he would do?" Moore responded unequivocally: "He would get us out of memories." A moment of silence passed before Grove made a startling proposal: "Why shouldn't you and I walk out that door, come back in, and do it ourselves?"

And that's what they did. But committing to a course of action is one thing; implementing it is another. Purging the social and cultural architecture that surrounded the DRAM business proved to be more difficult than making the choice had been.

R&D budget allocations were especially difficult. Moore, Grove, and other senior leaders hesitated, hemmed, hawed, wavered, compromised, and anguished over the transition. Despite their decision to discontinue production of the chips, DRAM continued to consume about one-third of Intel's total research budget. But by late 1984, they had succeeded in reducing DRAM production to a lone manufacturing site in Oregon—which proved to be an outpost of recalcitrance. To ensure cooperation, Grove had to replace the site manager. But the manager's replacement also attempted a compromise. Finally, Grove flew up to Oregon himself. With difficulty, he told the team there that Intel was discontinuing DRAM production permanently. He then directed his sales force to notify the company's memory customers that Intel would no longer make DRAMs.

The Risks of Equivocating

Looking back on the Intel episode, and on the aftermath of perhaps any difficult but necessary transition, there is no sensible argument for failing to make a move. But it always looks different in the heat of the moment's emotions.

Like Andy Grove and Gordon Moore, Zorn and her team at Longy, and now the board, had made known their convictions. The new vision unambiguously changed the identity of the school. Henceforth, teaching students to engage their communities through music would be Longy's primary purpose. Performance remained among key Longy's values, but now it was part of a bigger picture, serving as a necessary element through which classically trained musicians became great teachers or made a difference in the community. And now Zorn would have to steer that transformative vision into the teeth of a Cambridge-style gale.

Although we had surfaced and discussed the risks during the board meeting, they had not yet been fully realized. They would now become real and personal—never more so than with Longy's faculty, who would experience most keenly the consequential losses of the school's new mission. Zorn herself would feel the sting of the faculty's rebuke.

At first, like Grove and Moore, Zorn hedged. Many faculty members felt that Zorn wasn't merely changing Longy's identity; she was destroying it. The new strategy enfolded performance into the teaching mission, which challenged a hundred years of precedence. Given the faculty's natural desire to save their colleagues' part-time jobs, their vested interests in both community programming and established base of power, the new strategy provoked a powerful resistance. Faculty members were incredulous.

Two years later, Zorn was able to step back and see the reasoning behind their anger: "If you take away the apprenticeship ethic of performance, you lose this deep lineage." That lineage was part of the legacy of the faculty's own elite musicianship—it was how they had acquired their high level of skills. Also, of course, the planned changes to the community-program model meant that the faculty would lose what had been a highly effective market for their talents and interests. Looking back on her dealings with the faculty, Zorn now admits that she went through a period of trying to win over the very people most distressed by the changes she was bringing to Longy.

"I think I was inauthentic about it for some time. I used to say to faculty that Longy is about elite musicians, but then"— here Zorn mimes a small head fake to illustrate the dodge she was making—"also say that we were about teaching."

Presenting this spin began to take its toll. "It felt exhausting tailoring the message to different people. And it made me uncomfortable." Zorn's goal had been to persuade the faculty to buy into the future, to accept that what she was doing was right, but she couldn't do so unequivocally for fear of their reaction. "I was excited about the changes," she says. "But I was also afraid that they would think I was dumbing down the school. . . . So I modulated my language."

Zorn had been getting a lot of advice from people urging her not to alienate the faculty. "Everyone said I had to bring them along. They would say, 'Don't do things that will isolate you from the community. Don't scare them, don't make them anxious.' And on and on." So, following what seemed like good advice, Zorn continued to reason with her opponents, using language that managed to imply that the distance between them was smaller than, in reality, it was.

Appeasement is a risky strategy. In pursuing it, you become focused on satisfying your adversaries rather than moving forward with your allies. More important, it undermines what you think is the right thing to do. Compromise that is motivated by self-protection is what we had earlier dubbed "bad faith." But bad faith isn't just the prick of conscience you feel when equivocating; it has practical implications. As Zorn worked to keep the dialogue going, behind her back the faculty were discussing her ouster. "I would talk to the faculty, but what I didn't know was that they were saying, 'This isn't us. We've got to get her out of here!'"

What's the Right Thing to Do?

As her frustration mounted, it dawned on Zorn that her tactics weren't working. She had spent too much time with people who were implacably negative about the changes and too little time with those who were excited about them. That approach wasn't advancing the call she and others felt for the new mission. After a period of reflection, Zorn gave up taking advice and reacquainted herself with what she believed was the right thing to do.

In probably the most repeated and possibly the most important leadership aphorism ever uttered, Warren Bennis succinctly distilled the essence of leadership: "Managers do things right. Leaders do the right things." The creative act of figuring out and feeling responsible for determining what matters through the act of choice is an archetypal leadership experience.

As it happens, Shakespeare was particularly captivated by the burden of choice and deciding "right things." In the character of Henry V, he gives us one of his finest leadership lessons—very much like the one Karen Zorn was learning. Before the battle of Agincourt, in northern France, the young king Henry is paralyzed over the decision whether to send his beleaguered troops against the much larger French army that surrounds them on higher ground. He has so far received plenty of confusing advice from his princes and lords. And late in the night they urge him to join their council. Anguished, Henry declines their request, dons an old soldier's cloak, rubs dirt on his face, and goes out among his troops.

Around a campfire he encounters a group of three soldiers, who are discussing their own impending deaths and questioning the king's motives. The soldiers believe that the king is waging battle only for his own glory. Worse, they believe that if the fight goes badly—which, given the odds, it surely will—once the troops are slaughtered, Henry will simply ransom himself back to England (the customary recourse for royals and aristocrats). This talk angers Henry, who, still disguised as a common soldier, argues with the men. The confrontation so unsettles Henry that the young king asks himself larger questions about his own motives and whether the cause is sufficiently just to warrant risking the lives of his men. After working through these second thoughts, he concludes that the cause *is* just. He makes a leap of faith, delivers the famously inspiring Saint Crispin's Day speech—"We few, we happy few, we band of brothers"—and leads his army on to victory.

Beyond the high dramatics, Shakespeare makes the point that, in the end, choice is the act of believing in the right thing to do. In choosing, leaders must make themselves open to the uncertainties and risks of loss and then take responsibility for whatever happens. This brings us to the epicenter of the whole book and perhaps its most controversial proposal. An institutional identity crisis is, at heart, an ordeal centered around the denial of responsibility. It occurs when leaders disavow their responsibility for choosing.

Like Henry, Zorn made her move after coming to terms with "the right thing to do." After her emotional detour into the negativity of her opponents, she was able to reconnect with the positive energy of the changes that she and her team had proposed and the Longy board had adopted. In doing so, she regained what felt like high ground. "I gave up trying to convince the squeaky wheels. I realized that, whatever drove them, I couldn't satisfy it." She began spending more time with her allies and moved ahead with the strategy.

Though Zorn acted on her beliefs, the real world doesn't tend to wrap everything up neatly in a Saint Crispin's Day speech. For Longy, there were legal battles yet to be waged. The faculty formed a union and went to court. In October 2010, the General Counsel of the National Labor Relations Board (NLRB) issued, on behalf of the union, a formal complaint against Longy for unfair labor practices. The NLRB asserted that Longy had a duty to engage the union in "effects bargaining" with respect to the impact of the faculty realignment, and moreover that the school was required to bargain with faculty about the decision itself. In its ruling, however, the court determined that Longy was under no duty to bargain about its decision, although the judge stated that Longy should have offered faculty an opportunity to bargain over the criteria for realignment. The court's ruling brought Longy and the faculty back into discussion. Following negotiations, a settlement and collective bargaining agreement were finally reached in early 2011. The union withdrew all charges filed with the NLRB. Reparations were made, and the community healed. A year later, rather remarkably, Zorn would receive a commendation from the faculty union, supporting her and Longy's vision for the future.

A Fortuitous Meeting

In the heat of battle, it can often be almost impossible to look ahead, past the turmoil of the moment, to the benefits that will flow from achieving clarity. As we saw with Intel's stubborn devotion to DRAM chips, the anxiety in the foreground becomes gigantic and obscures the gains to be made on the horizon. But eventually you move past it, arriving at the harvest that transformation can bring. Longy's transformation would yield results that neither Zorn nor anybody else could imagine.

While Zorn was preparing for the big board meeting and feeling more confident that Longy could implement a turnaround on its own, she learned that Lesley University had decided against a merger. Around that time, a member of the board encouraged Zorn to meet with Leon Botstein, the conductor of the American Symphony Orchestra and president of Bard College. Coincidentally, the board member's sister happened to be on the board at Bard. Her sister had similarly suggested to Botstein that he meet Zorn.

Zorn agreed to have lunch with Botstein, not knowing quite what to expect. "I figured that Leon is a smart guy, maybe he can give me some good advice." Botstein, known for his inventiveness, became the youngest U.S. college president in 1970, at the age of twenty-three, when he took over New Hampshire's Franconia College. In 1975, he moved to Bard, a selective liberal arts college in upstate New York with a strong music heritage.

At lunch, Botstein peppered Zorn with questions. "He was fascinated with where I grew up and how I got to the East Coast." Botstein was interested in people who had grown up around the Midwest and retained the Midwestern work ethic but had been irresistibly drawn eastward, to the heart of music culture.

Then Botstein asked about Longy. By this time, Zorn had completely internalized the story. "I was able for the first time to really say where we were heading." She shared with him her conviction that music education in America needed to change, and that the key to that was to educate performers to be excellent teachers.

Botstein grew animated. He shared her feeling for the problem. He compared poor music instruction to the difficulty that math teachers had who weren't mathematicians. They might know the textbook well enough, but they lack the passion and understanding needed to go beyond the lesson plan and connect students with the foundational ideas. He liked the direction in which Zorn was leading Longy. "That's what I've wanted to do," he told her. "We do wonderful things at Bard, but we haven't been able to make an impact on public-school music education."

Then, out of the blue, he said, "We should merge!"

It was a daring invitation. But remarkably, the proposal held. Over the next few years—eventually under the new banner of the Longy School of Music *of Bard College*—Zorn and Botstein began to build innovative new programs across the country

One of these programs came to be known as *Take a Stand*. For a number of years, Zorn had been closely watching the radically innovative music teaching called El Sistema. Many in the United States had come to know El Sistema through the famous Venezuelan-born conductor Gustavo Dudamel, music director of the Los Angeles Philharmonic. The exuberant, wild-haired Dudamel had been the subject of a *60 Minutes* segment that featured his involvement with El Sistema at an early age. The method, originally developed by Dr. Jose Antonio Abreu, had been developed in Venezuela to train children—many from the poorest barrios—in classical music. It was a way to lift children up out of the deadening context of poverty by using music as a source of hope, inspiration, and constructive distraction.

Zorn clearly saw the link between El Sistema and the kind of educational reform Longy was pursuing with Bard. With Botstein's encouragement she reached out to Deborah Borda, president and chief executive officer of the Los Angeles Philharmonic. It wasn't long before Bard, Longy, and the Los Angeles Philharmonic had forged a three-way partnership to launch social change through music. Suddenly, Longy was making upbeat news—no longer about labor disputes—not only in the *Boston Globe* but also in the *Guardian* and other far-flung media.

None of these fortuitous events were coincidental. To the contrary, they were the direct result of Longy's commitment to its purpose and hard-won clarity, and of Karen Zorn's transformation into the kind of leader who was able to make difficult choices anchored in guiding principles. Like her father, she had learned to value doing the right thing over being liked. She had found her place to stand.

When I asked her recently why she thought doors had begun to open for Longy, she said she believed it was "because we had found our purpose, and an authentic way to tell our story. It found resonance with other people who wanted the same things. It wouldn't have happened without all the work. I didn't make a *pitch* to Leon. I was simply telling it like it was." Zorn told me that she used to try to calculate what donors wanted to hear from her so that she could tailor her message to their interests. "But now we have this story. If it resonates, that's great; and if it doesn't, then that's okay."

There have been other gains. Prospective faculty now clearly understand Longy's mission. "They see that we're trying to get folks to teach differently," says Zorn. "They get it. The musicians now applying to be faculty are knocking our socks off! The word is out—we would not have gotten those people five years ago." The school is also doing a better job of competing for students. "We have ten students now deciding between Longy and Yale. You wouldn't have seen that five years ago either."

Finally, it's worth noting the irony that the assets that Longy most feared losing—its reputation and faculty—have now become more visible and highly regarded than they were before, when the school's mission was stuck in the murky middle. Based on Longy's experience, it is worth remembering that in the shadow of an unmade decision the focal points of fear seem so much larger than they turn out to be in reality. At Intel, the senior team was terrified of the customer response to its proposed exit from the DRAM market. Indeed, that worry prolonged the company's period of denial. But, as Andy Grove later recalled, "[the customers'] reaction was, for all practical purposes, benign." One customer, he said, even joked, "Well, it sure took you a long time!" After liberating the capital and management energy to pursue microprocessors, Intel took off like a rocket. "We became the largest semiconductor company in the world," said Grove, "larger even than the Japanese companies that had beaten us in memories. By now, our identification with microprocessors is so strong that it's difficult for us to get noticed for our other products."

As time passed, Longy's path led to unpredictable destinations. To be sure, Longy has had genuine success. But the school has also faced more tough decisions. In the spring of 2013—two months before this book went to press—Longy announced a decision that would have been unimaginable back in 2009. In order to accommodate the growing number of conservatory students jostling for limited rehearsal space, the school communicated to the press, its students, and the Cambridge community that effective August 2013 Longy would no longer continue community programming. Undoubtedly the children and families whose lives were enriched by those programs will experience this decision as a tragic loss. Yet by allocating scarce resources to the conservatory, Longy kept its commitment to train degree-seeking students. It acted with purpose. From our vantage point, the decision is also an illustration of one of the main themes in this book. It is a sober reminder that whether we like it or not, choice is naturally accompanied by loss. In order to affirm one purpose we must often diminish another.

The Freedom of Choosing

The philosopher, playwright, and literary critic Jean Paul Sartre once said, "We are our choices." Choices define us. It was this reason that existentialists like Sartre often wrote about anxiety, dread, and anguish. They understood that momentous choices provoke such powerful emotions because the stakes are high. Choosing requires a good measure of courage. It requires taking a stand.

Although the existentialists were principally concerned with the struggle of individuals to find meaning in life, the collective environment of a business is as good a place as any in which to see that struggle play out. Leaders have the burden of making choices for the benefit of the institutions they lead and the people who work in them.

I am sure that by now you have gotten a sense of, on one hand, the costs of not choosing, and on the other, the gains to be made by seizing the day. And you have a sense of how the act of choosing works. Choices test us. They generate anxiety strong enough to tempt us to avoid the act of choosing altogether. Yet strangely enough, the anxiety, once faced, can become a source of vitality. The first great existentialist philosopher, Søren Kierkegaard, knew this; he argued that the anxiety of commitment is really the fundamental stuff of life.

Our choices disclose who we are. They are what gives us identity: they say "Here's who I am; this is what I'm up to." The difficulty with choice is inherently related to the gains to be made by identity and purpose. This is why Kierkegaard called the anxiety surrounding a self-defining choice the "dizziness of freedom." In my work with executives, I have come to believe the relationship between purpose, choice, anxiety, and identity applies to collective spheres like business as much as to individuals. Leaders vanquish the disorienting and frightening feelings associated with choice *only when* they finally accept the responsibility of choosing, both for themselves and the organization.

The primary responsibility of leadership, then, is to take responsibility. Choice, to be made authentically, must be formed from the leader's ability to own the burden that accompanies power. Paul at Dividio seemed unable to free himself from the burden he would have to place on his colleagues, even though he knew redefining the business was the right thing to do. Intel's Andy Grove and Gordon Moore vacillated and temporized on the way to making their leap of faith. And Zorn allowed herself, for a time, to become too immersed in the faculty's objections to her new strategy. Ultimately she freed herself to do the right thing.

When we embrace choice, we gain clarity of purpose. It is the resounding clarity—wrought by commitment—that ultimately severs the Gordian knot of an identity crisis. As Zorn learned, this defining commitment also gives an organization its distinctiveness in the marketplace and a feeling of coherence and integrity. It gives the organization a story to tell. The clarity attracts others, like Leon Botstein of Bard, who seek similar purposes. Even as customers we may feel that a company is "special." Distinctive organizations—of which there are relatively few—seem to radiate purpose, and we get it. You can bet that behind that specialness is a leader who faced anxiety and risk in order to take a stand on the business.

Of course, you don't have to be customer or a leader to understand the impact of this kind of choice. Many of us are fortunate enough to work in a special organization. The organization is up to something, and you can feel it. As we'll see in the next chapter, a well-made choice can endow an enterprise with meaning, identity, and a sense of community.

6

The Hunger for Purpose

A few months ago, my colleagues at Pivot and I designed a leadership-development project for a cohort of up-and-coming PayPal leaders. Among the things I learned from the experience—described in more detail shortly—is how important it is for the people of an enterprise to feel that their work is guided by a shared central purpose. Purpose provides a sense of community and a point of orientation—a North Star, if you will. It is the institutional equivalent of a charismatic individual's point of view. The value employees place on purpose can outrank even the importance they place on money.

It is easy to be skeptical of such a claim. Money is typically presumed to have the strongest hold on people's motivations. And, without question, financial rewards are right up there. But interesting research suggests that people are often more deeply driven by other factors.

Take for example the recent research on how professionals actually experience work. Harvard Business School's Professor Teresa M. Amabile and research partner Steven J. Kramer spent more than a decade studying what they called the "inner

work lives" of 238 knowledge workers. Each day, the participants were asked to write about a single memorable event,
using the classic form of a diary entry. Amabile and Kramer
chronicled their findings—based on more than twelve thousand of the subjects' diary entries—in a May 2007 *Harvard
Business Review* article ("Inner Work Life: Understanding the
Subtext of Business Performance"). The authors' rich trove of
data gave a rare glimpse into unseen factors that influence
employees' productivity and their attitudes about work. The
themes extracted from these entries were striking. A great
many of the professionals in the study often experienced
intense and disturbing emotions at work—frustration, disdain,
and even disgust.

Amabile and Kramer found that such emotions were quite
common and that they had a demonstrable impact on the
performance, creativity, and energy people brought to their
work. As described in a *New York Times* piece on their research,
the authors identified "an inner work life system," characterized by a fluid "interplay among perceptions, emotions, and
motivations" that determined these positive or negative
experiences.[1]

In terms of motivation, what employees valued most—
more than money, more than perks, and more than status—
was the feeling that they were "moving forward" and achieving
meaningful goals. "When we compared people's best days with
their worst," Amabile had told the *New York Times*, "the most
important differentiator was being able to make progress in
the work."

Though the evidence gathered by Amabile and Kramer
focused mainly on project work of a technical kind, it was clear

that participants felt most adrift and least happy when they were given too little guidance to know whether they were succeeding or not, and to what end. Conversely, they were happiest when they understood the assignment, the progress they were making, and how their work fit in the larger scheme of the project's ultimate goals.

It is not a great leap to conclude from this research that people in a workplace have a strong desire to feel that they are part of something larger than themselves. They want to know not only why they are doing what they do; they also want to know how it fits with others' contributions as part of the whole endeavor. In short, they strive to understand the context of their work—its meaning and its purpose. As Fredrick Nietzsche famously said, "He who has a *why* can endure any *how*."

Creating Meaning at PayPal

The cohort of up-and-coming PayPal leaders I spoke of earlier had been tasked by the firm's top executives to take a deep, outside-in look at three core customer groups. The group had split up into three teams and had been working energetically to make sense of what they'd learned from customers. The teams had spent a significant amount of time in the field, doing ethnographic research on the needs and lives of potential customers. Based on analysis of the results, each team created a prototype new value proposition and business model for their targeted customers. They had already shared an earlier draft of this output with some of the company's stakeholders. Now they were ready to present a further-refined version to PayPal's top executive group.

In a sense, this was the leadership-development project's final exam.

While the teams prepared for their big presentations, I took the executive group—including PayPal's president, David Marcus—into another room. This event was an opportunity for them to affirm the tone and culture of the business for some of their most promising future leaders. I wanted to make sure they had thought through how they wanted to engage the group. When we had finished and were leaving the conference room, we heard a loud roar coming from the ballroom down the hall—shouting, cheers, and hand-clapping. As we entered, the nineteen members of the three teams were all on their feet, greeting the executives with whooping, hollering applause.

The enthusiastic display was distinctly un-PayPal-like behavior. Public exuberance is not one of PayPal's defining characteristics. So as the executives took their seats at the front of the room, they seemed a bit startled by the new and different mood on display.

Once the teams began their presentations, it was clear that their members had been through a transformative experience. They told powerful stories about encounters they had had with customers. For example, one team had been perplexed about how to penetrate the Indian market. One day, meeting with an Indian family of seven who lived in a cramped apartment in Chennai, the team discovered that the family used their old-styled functional mobile phones for myriad aspects of daily life, including to make payments. And this was despite the fact that most Indians don't have smartphones or continuous Internet access. Still, their phones were the dominant interface for financial interactions. Therefore phones would have to be the primary medium for PayPal in that market. Another team recounted the frustrations of small business owners—one of PayPal's traditional constituencies—because they ended up spending more time managing inventory, doing accounting, and dealing with payments than they did interacting with customers.

The teams made bold calls for PayPal to rethink its approach to customers by becoming more of a resource and problem-solver. They also shared their feelings of exhilaration and camaraderie at having worked together as teams. The presentations were so passionately and earnestly delivered that by the time they ended, two executives were seen to be holding back tears (more un-PayPal-like behavior).

In a lengthy discussion after the presentation concluded, team members discussed their struggles, their progress, the sense of purpose they had found, and the meaning they'd created for themselves by working to solve customers' problems. The executives wanted to know how they might transfer the ingredients of this relatively limited experience to the broader PayPal community. President David Marcus sent me this email that night with a poignant reflection: "Today was truly one of the highest points of my life at PayPal. Seeing these individuals form such powerful teams was amazing. And, more importantly, seeing [their] growth and the quality of their output was mind-boggling."

Based on what I later heard, it was a watershed experience for many in the room. But, oddly enough, I had mixed feelings. Certainly, I was proud to have been a part of what happened. At Pivot, our job is to create the conditions that make transformative changes possible. But I also felt a measure of sadness over how few and far between such meaningful experiences are. Why don't they happen more often?

Why Corporate Life So Often Disappoints

In truth, people have lamented the loss of meaning and relatedness in organizations for a very long time. Max Weber, an early-twentieth-century sociologist, used the word "disenchantment" to describe the loss of meaning that accompanies the rationalization and bureaucratization of modern organizational life. Weber argued that institutions had once been places where individuals channeled their energy into action that promoted cohesion and collective identity, even spirituality. But modern industrial organizations replaced those earlier, more human businesses with an "iron cage" of efficiency and routine.

I think that we have left behind the era of the iron cage—our systems are now more fluid, more fragmented, and less hierarchical and routinized than in Weber's day. This is especially the case for those in the knowledge professions, where work environments feel less like overly organized bureaucracies than like loosely organized anarchy. But disenchantment remains a disease in contemporary businesses of all kinds. You get a sense of this when—as Amabile and Kramer did—you ask people to step back and reflect on their work experiences.

I once coached an extremely accomplished man named Jonathan who had been a partner at McKinsey and a senior executive at a number of large banks and technology companies. One day, he asked me the kind of question to which one doesn't necessarily expect an answer: "Why does corporate life suck so much?" When I remained silent, Jonathan went on:

"Does it *have* to be soul-sucking? I've never met a corporation that hasn't been that way. I'm not talking about never having a bad day, but I want a place that *inspires* me. Maybe I'm an outlier. Maybe others don't care. But to me it just doesn't seem right."

People like Jonathan are not "outliers" by any means. They may even constitute a kind of silent majority in corporations these days. And their plight is among the reasons I decided to write this book. Many of the organizations I encounter lack the charisma that comes from identifying with a larger cause.

Sadly, the loss of shared purpose makes the experience of business feel as though it's every man or woman for him- or herself. People who feel disconnected from the primary task of the business become isolated from one another. They work for a paycheck or to gain new skills before the next, more promising career move comes along. In sum, when people are disenchanted they tend to treat the organization instrumentally, like a marketplace that exists to satisfy their own needs. Yes, these values can motivate hard work, but they don't fully compensate for what is missing. This leaves people disenfranchised, in a sense, from the possibility of meaning and the rewards of working in a business that feels like it has a guiding purpose.

My friend Larry Hirschhorn has suggested that this loss of meaning and purpose damages the esprit de corps of the business because it leads to *indifference*.[2] When we treat our workplaces instrumentally, as a market for meeting our own needs, we tend to treat people in the organization that way too. I once coached a manager whose favorite metaphor for work was a bank. Every time he did something helpful for a colleague, he treated the favor like a transaction. His job, he said, was to accumulate credits in his "favor bank" that he could cash in for returned favors at some future point. At its best, instrumentality may lead to reciprocity of a kind. But it also degrades relationships. That's because markets are based on transactions, not relationships. In relationships concern is for the other. In market transactions concern is for the self. The old maxim *Caveat emptor*, or "buyer beware," applies in markets. The maxim encapsulates the basic wisdom that you cannot trust the seller; you have to apply due diligence so as to verify that you are not being taken advantage of. Writ large, the problem with caveat emptor is that it leads to chronic concerns about self-protection or whether we are "one up" or "one down" to our colleagues and/or employers. "It's a jungle out there," we may say. People who feel indifferent and instrumental assume the same about others. But in business, where most of us have thousands of interactions with others, caveat emptor isn't just alienating; it's exhausting.

As Jonathan insisted to me, it shouldn't be that way. Clearly, he wasn't someone who shrank from the challenges and frustrations of hard work. What was missing for him was the sense of belonging to an enterprise with significance beyond himself. You can think of what's missing as the Higgs boson particle of corporate matter—the glue that turns individual wage earners into a cohesive community guided by a shared sense of purpose.

Connecting with the Why of Business

I was discussing this question of purpose with my friend Lew McCreary, a writer and editor who helped me immensely as I was writing this book. We were talking about the meaning we get from work, and Lew told me the story of how, in 1987, he joined the staff of a soon-to-launch magazine for chief information officers—the super-enhanced C-suite version of what used to be the IT guy.

On his way to a Red Sox game, McCreary stopped off to meet the magazine's founding editor for dinner at a Chinese restaurant near Fenway Park. "Because I was trying to get to the game, she gave me this really quick elevator pitch while we were eating pot stickers and egg rolls," recalled McCreary. "The pitch was basically that, because technology was becoming so important, businesses needed the folks who ran their technology function to transform themselves from introverted geeks into highly influential, tech-savvy strategists."

The purpose revealed in that pitch wasn't saving the world, but it was clear and had meaning. "The way she described it was sort of like frogs turning into princes," said McCreary. 'They're being asked to do something incredibly difficult. The skills they're going to need are totally different from the skills they have. So huge numbers of them are going to fail. But if the magazine does what it's supposed to do, we can make a difference by helping some of them succeed.'

"To me, that sounded like an important mission. I completely imprinted on her pitch: *Oh my god, these people are so screwed! But we can help them cheat death!* I don't remember who won the Red Sox game, but I totally remember feeling that I wanted to be part of that magazine."

Once the magazine launched, readers quickly developed a durable loyalty to it (twenty-five years later, it was still going strong). "They valued the fact that we were in their corner, were their advocate and counselor. Over the years, I kept repeating that elevator pitch to new hires. And every year it became more demonstrably true—a lot of CIOs *did* fail. And that made our mission incredibly important to our readers."

It also gave McCreary and his colleagues striking clarity. "To have a workplace grow out of something like that drove a remarkably low level of politics and distraction, and a remarkably high level of shared consensus around knowing what our purpose was."

Purpose is the "why" of any business. When leaders fail to make fundamental choices, the identity crisis that ensues corrodes the organization's purpose, thereby undermining its ability to create meaning and a sense of community. McCreary's story illustrates that the reverse is also true: a choice wholeheartedly embraced creates clarity of purpose. This has both internal and external ramifications. As we saw in the Longy example, doors open for an organization that can tell its own story with conviction. Its people can live and work passionately rather than drift as lone free agents, making it up as they go along. Purpose provides meaning, motivation, and community to a business.

Meaning That Makes Sense

In Norman Mailer's gargantuan spy novel, *Harlot's Ghost*, one of his characters, inspired by the spy fiction she read in her youth, pursues a career in the CIA. The job lands her in exactly the sorts of dramatic situations that she had so loved reading about. But over time she discovers that her role in the job is only a bit part. Instead of experiencing the full arc of the plot, she does a small turn in the middle chapters. Having missed the beginning of the story and its end, she feels deeply unsatisfied. Mailer uses her experience to make the point that underneath it all people want to feel as if they are a part of an unfolding story that gives them meaning, but that this kind of relationship to the whole is terrifically hard to come by.

Mailer reflected on why it's so critical to be part of the bigger story: "Often, one did not learn how it all turned out. That struck me as being about what life is like: The gun over the mantelpiece does not often get fired. We live in and out of ongoing plots every day of our lives, but they are discontinuous. Our love of plot . . . comes out of our need to find the chain of cause and effect that so often is missing in our own existence."[3]

I would argue that an organization's purpose—embedded as it is in a narrative of how a business solves a problem—brings together the fragmented collection of characters and events that our work lives comprise. Purpose coheres, unifies, and gives meaning to our experiences. Purpose makes sense of things and allows us to feel a part of something bigger than ourselves.

Meaning also helps us make sense of the world around us. It makes things intelligible by putting order into an otherwise chaotic world. Karl Weick, a professor at the Ross School of Business (University of Michigan), has written extensively about sense-making in business organizations. He makes use of an apparently true story told in a poem by Czech scientist and poet Nobel Laureate Miroslav Holub. The poem recounts the fate of a reconnaissance team that gets hopelessly lost in the Alps during a snowstorm. For two days there is no sign of the unit, and the lieutenant who dispatched them fears that he has sent the men to their graves. But on the third day they miraculously appear. They tell the lieutenant that, just as they had reached the point of despair and the certainty that they were done for, one of the men discovered a forgotten map folded up in his pocket. Map in hand, they pitched camp and waited out the storm. When it was over, they used the map to get their bearings and find their way back.

The astonished lieutenant asked to see this extraordinary map. After closely examining it, he discovered that the map was not of the Alps, but of the Pyrenees.

Weick argued that the value of the map to the group of lost soldiers had nothing to do with accuracy. In order to take some action to survive, the soldiers needed to feel like they could make sense of where they were and where they were going. For this purpose, even the wrong map is better than no map at all. Or, as strategy specialists have been known to say, "Even the wrong strategy is better than none."

In order to take action we need to make the world reasonably intelligible. Most organizations these days are remarkably unintelligible—chaotic, fragmented, and ambiguous. We tend to celebrate flat, decentralized, networked structures and robust strategies that allow us to be many things to many people. Today's "fast company" is advised to accept ambiguity as the acceptable norm rather than resist it.

The unacknowledged truth is that our contemporary approach to business carries a steep price. The human need for order and sense may seem outdated in today's fast, fluid world, but although business has changed, human beings have not. Yes, long-range planning is often obsolete before the ink dries and even Weick's map is of little use when the ground below us shifts. But there must still be some constant, some North Star to help guide people's actions. Purpose—and the meaning it confers—is an antidote to relentless mutability of contemporary business. Purpose orients the enterprise in relation to its world—especially important when the terrain is undergoing change and when the pace of change is accelerating at unpredictable speeds. Paradoxically, agility—that most sought-after capability these days—comes not from opportunism, expediency, or being everything to everyone, but by being grounded in a sense of purpose that allows a company to develop a point of view about the world. We need a North Star when the ground on which we tread is uncertain and changing.

Meaning and intelligibility wrought by purpose let us know what matters—what counts as being important and what doesn't. When I work with senior managers, one of the biggest issues they often share with me is the lack of clear priorities in their organization. Everything is important, and therefore nothing is important. This flattening of value is paralyzing because it diminishes the organization's ability to make trade-offs between one activity and another, making it next to impossible for employees to reliably judge "what has significance for us." As Longy's leaders relearned, not every area of the business can be treated as equal; some matter more than others. A clear understanding of these differences helps everyone know when to say yes, when to say no, what to pursue, and what to let go of.

The ability to make these calculations is ever more critical in today's business environment, where certainty is rare and there is an unrelenting barrage of choices. We are pulled this way and that. We waver, compromise, and hesitate. The waves of choices inhibit action and forward progress. They paralyze. Alternatively, we go along to get along, often taking the path of least resistance, or we do what we can to keep our head down. This is a world of CYA where we end up making choices whose sole purpose is to delicately balance conflicting interpretations of value in the business. This leads to a work life of fragmentation, frustration, and ambiguity—an experience of work without purpose.

Purpose—the core or "why" of an enterprise—provides a basis for discriminating. It is a guide for helping us decide what counts. When purpose is clear, and is both shared and supported, business operates from a secure foundation that enables people to take action.

Why Meaning Motivates

The meaning we gain from purpose provides orientation and intelligibility; it also motivates. Meaning is the inner experience of being inspired by purpose.

On October 19, 1944, the Nazis sent a young Jewish doctor named Viktor Frankl, along with his new bride, Tilly, age twenty-four, and other family members, to Auschwitz. There, Frankl was processed and transported to the concentration camp at Dachau, where he came down with typhoid fever. Frankl resisted collapse by reconstructing a lost manuscript, which he had written before the war, on slips of paper he stole from the concentration camp's office. In April 1945, Americans liberated Dachau. Frankl returned to Vienna only to learn that

Tilly and his mother and brother had been murdered in Auschwitz.

In trying to make sense of what had happened, Frankl spoke to many other concentration camp survivors. He came to believe that the people who staved off despair and survived the camps' horrific circumstances were those who—as he did at Dachau by reconstructing his manuscript—had been able to create meaning in their lives. Frankl went on to write *Man's Search for Meaning*, one of the twentieth century's most influential books in psychology and philosophy, which argued that the prime motive of human behavior is to create meaning and purpose.

Since Frankl's insight, researchers have busied themselves more deeply with the question of what motivates us and enables us to thrive and lead a happy life. As noted earlier, psychologists have discovered that money is not always the most powerful motivator of performance. For example, although monetary rewards tend to increase performance with simple repetitive tasks, psychologists have found that financial incentives actually diminish performance when work requires creativity and problem solving, particularly in ambiguous situations.[4] Carrots and sticks have their limitations.

It's not just a matter of performance. Purpose is linked to well-being. Young professionals who aspire to and achieve purpose-driven goals in life tend to be more satisfied, experiencing lower anxiety and less depression than those who achieve extrinsic goals such as wealth, fame, or status. Indeed, research shows that people who seek and then achieve extrinsic goals tend to have *more* anxiety and depression.[5] Even the physiology of the human brain seems to thrive on purpose. In a recent report in the archives of general psychiatry of the *Journal of the American Medical Association*, researchers found that elderly people who scored high on a sense-of-purpose scale—who had a "tendency to derive meaning from life's experiences and to possess a sense of intentionality and goal directedness that guides behavior"—were 2.4 times likelier to avoid Alzheimer's disease than people with low scores. This was true even when researchers factored in demographics, social surroundings, socioeconomic factors, and other psychiatric symptoms.[6]

Indeed, beyond a necessary threshold for livability, money may be a rather poor substitute for purpose. The infamous Black Monday (described in the preceding chapter) when fifteen star microprocessor innovators left Intel is a good reminder that the most creative, high-performing employees—the real problem-solvers—are precisely the ones most powerfully motivated by the business's larger purpose—and most profoundly demotivated when purpose wavers or is lacking.

To make this point even more personal, consider the following comment made by a high performer on his way out of a business I was working with:

> I've been thinking a lot about this. There are several
> factors that drove my decision to leave. At one time,
> this was a company I thought I would *not* leave. But
> the business is confused now. I think we're having an
> identity crisis. There are a number of reasons as to
> why this is happening. I mean, the people here are
> tremendous, so it's not a talent issue. I think that the
> business is just too spread out. Our core business
> requires an amazing amount of focus and creativity,

but the non-core stuff is increasingly a distraction. I don't know what the latest figures are. . . . Maybe half or a third of the business is outside of the core—but it's rudderless. It languishes on the vine, even though we still have to water it. I wish instead that we could go back to our roots. But right now, the brand does not have the vitality, the energy. Not just from the outside but from inside. And that is the reason I'm leaving.

Why is the meaning created by purpose so essential to motivation in business? Larry Hirschhorn puts the answer succinctly: "Passion," he says, "derives from the experience of incompleteness."[7] One could argue that all human beings have a feeling of being incomplete, that something is missing for them that they need to fill in order to feel whole. When that something is missing, we seek to restore the balance—often with a sense of urgency and energy focused on doing great work. This is what it means to be driven.

That said, we can satisfy what's missing in our lives in two very different ways:

1. If the business presents us with a larger opportunity for purpose, we internalize the work of the enterprise and make it our own—our work helps us feel whole.
2. However, if we lack the outlet provided by a purposeful enterprise, we instead exploit the organization for personal gain. The business becomes a setting in which we maximize our own personal interests.

That second instrumental type of organization feels shallow. It lacks the depth and richness that make work rewarding for us as individuals. Worse, its shallowness exacts a severe penalty on the community of the business. The lack of shared purpose promotes indifference toward the primary task of the business *and* toward one's colleagues. People who feel indifferent themselves project it onto their peers. Trust frays. Such an environment tempts us to focus on self-protection and self-advancement, to feel an excessive concern about our status relative to others, and to display a knee-jerk alertness to being taken advantage of. In short, indifference and instrumentality are the most corrosive version of office politics: at Apple, Donna Dubinsky, feeling dissed, squares off against Debi Coleman; CNN's New York "celebrities" ridicule their "inbred" colleagues in Atlanta; and the managers gathered in a ballroom snort and roll their eyes over their leaders' failure of nerve.

Naturally, businesses lost in a crisis are going to suffer in myriad ways. And—just to put things in perspective—these problems arise because leaders fail to understand the extraordinary power they could activate by making a choice and taking a stand on the business.

Think what happened when the Apple story I recounted at the start of this book finally circled back to Steve Jobs's return to Apple. During his exile in the not-quite-wilderness of Next Computer and Pixar, Jobs clearly learned from his mistakes. His pirate inclinations—which had riven the company he and Steve Wozniak started, pitting divisions against one another—had been tamed. Given a second chance, he was determined to be a uniter, not a divider. Upon his return, Apple was unified by a vision that featured the innovation of stunning elegance applied equally to product designs and business models. Ironically, the result was worthy of John Sculley's image of a soaring cathedral, which Donna Dubinsky had found so incongruous with the reality of 1985.

Cause and Community

Purpose engenders meaning, motivation, and, finally, community. The hunger for purpose is within ourselves, but its object lies beyond us. "Success, like happiness, cannot be pursued," said Viktor Frankl; "it must ensue . . . as the unintended side effect of *one's personal dedication to a course greater than oneself*" (my emphasis). To be sure, each of us have our own sense of purpose, but it's a yearning that can be satisfied only in community with others. We serve ourselves by serving a cause that is larger than us alone. By bringing us together, purpose counteracts the prospect of alienation, loneliness, frustration, and aimlessness that all people, perhaps especially in business, are prone to in its absence.

A business without purpose lacks energy, urgency, and the bright horizon toward which a community might navigate. This lack is felt as a persistent awareness that something is broken but you can't figure out what it is. This is the "problem with no name" in organizational life.

To understand the loss, imagine for a moment the alternative—a purpose-filled organization. This is a company that is galvanized, productive, and possibly even happy. The company is successful, its employees engaged, the different parts of the business aligned around a shared purpose. The culture is vibrant, and people have confidence in leadership and in themselves as instruments, not of egoistic gain, but of the larger purpose. Problems get solved. Plans are made and executed. One may even sense a pervasive *esprit de corps* throughout the business—even when times are difficult.

Roch Parayre, an instructor at the Wharton School of Business with whom I frequently partner, tells the story of an encounter he had at a Southwest Airlines customer service counter after a cancelled flight. As passengers lined up to rebook their flights, a man at the front began yelling at the Southwest gate agent that the flight cancellation had made him miss the most important meeting of his life. He became so unpleasant that the young woman behind the counter peered at him and said in a voice clearly loud enough for others to hear, "Sir, if you don't settle down right this instant I'm going to jump over this counter, bend you over my knee, and spank you like a baby!" She did this with authority, but also with a wink and a smile. The rest of the passengers applauded, and the man—rebuked but not shamed—smiled sheepishly and calmed down.

Now, it's possible to attribute the Southwest gate agent's assertiveness to her own unique personality. But it's also very likely that she felt *authorized* to do what she did. It fit within the purpose and personality of the airline. That she did it with such good humor suggests that the organizational values gave her permission and even encouragement to enact, in a small way, the culture of the business.

Southwest's identity and purpose are resoundingly simple. "Southwest Airlines is family-like, which implies love," said CEO Gary Kelly.[8] In a world of highly polished, professional-ized public images, Southwest's stock ticker symbol is LUV, and their logo features a corny heart. Southwest often plays with this identity, tweaking their rivals, as in the amusing "bags fly free" television commercials. Notice that their ads don't feature the CEO or a celebrity spokesperson. Instead, there's a group of good-natured bag handlers. Watching Southwest commercials, you feel the apparently sincere satisfaction those employees derive out of doing the right thing for customers.

Now, you could say that an airline, given its primarily frontline customer contact, is more likely than other industries to have employees eagerly focused on enjoying the benefits of purpose. Guess again. To make a case for the universality of the hunger for purpose, I want to wrap up with one last story. It is set in an industry most of us would consider least likely to be preoccupied with meaning and purpose: Wall Street banking.

Fighting for Clarity

In 2012, I directed a leadership experience for the one hundred senior managers of a large financial institution, which I will call Tabernia to protect confidentiality. Tabernia has an impressive footprint: with many billions of dollars under management, it is one of the world's biggest banks. Needless to say, leadership matters in an institution of this size and influence.

Tabernia was getting back its sea legs by the summer of 2012. The financial crisis of 2008, and the resulting long-term decline of interest rates, had hit the bank hard. Many of the bank's core products and services had long been augmented with related premium offerings that drove healthy profit margins. However, in the post-collapse world, demand for those offerings had sharply declined. The problem was clear:

revenues were declining as costs continued to rise. So in 2011, the bank began to change its business model.

I met Tabernia's senior managers for a four-day leadership program in a large conference hall in upstate New York. Among the participants were CEO Jim Nolan and the bulk of his executive team. The objective of the work was to help ready the team to deal with ongoing transformation, as the bank overhauled the way it provided services to its clients.

The first day and a half of the experience were devoted to innovation, rethinking strategy, and stress-testing the emerging strategy against different competitive scenarios. It didn't take long for me to figure out that something wasn't quite right. Hands kept flying up. People were confused about the direction of the company. *What was this change?* they wanted to know. *Was it to be a handful of limited initiatives or an entirely new strategy to change the company?*

By the evening of the second day, the program had begun to go off the rails. The group was less interested in training than in understanding where the bank was headed. The program wouldn't continue successfully unless the group got some clarity about the future from its top leaders. Against the possibility of an uprising, we called an audible. We invited the group to take out a piece of paper and do two simple things:

1. Write down the questions they wanted Nolan and the top team to answer on the following day.
2. Give the executive team counsel about how to address the group.

The two questions yielded a hundred or so participant responses, which we consolidated into six pages of comments for Nolan and his team. The group hadn't pulled any punches—many of the comments were strongly worded. A significant majority focused on Tabernia's vision: "What is it? Why are we doing it?" "Spell it out for us. Be honest—lose the rose-colored-glasses approach." "You keep saying we need 22 percent margin, but that's just a number, it doesn't mean anything." As Dubinsky had done, the group called out the confusions and contradictions they saw in the emerging business model. They wanted to know which activities or business lines, under any proposed new strategy, they would have to let go of. "Tell us what *not* to do!" said one participant. "If we want to be the 'investments experts to the world,' that sounds like we're being all things to all people," said another.

Collectively, the group's comments were a major truth-to-power moment. Nolan's leadership team spent five hours that afternoon categorizing the comments and preparing its response. They even counted the number of times certain key words appeared ("vision" appeared fifty-one times, "communication" forty-two).

By the next morning, it was as if a dam were about to burst. Ironically, I was in the midst of teaching a session about purpose—the very thing they were seeking. One by one, hands went up. Attendees challenged me. Fingers wagged. People were impatient—and indignant. As the authority figure in the room, I was a perfect proxy for Nolan. As such, I took some direct hits. In short order, it turned into full revolt and things began to unravel. The group wanted Nolan, and I was not Nolan. On day four of the program, they'd had enough of my teaching. The leadership they really wanted was from their own colleagues.

I will pause here to note that not a single comment from the Tabernia senior managers mentioned compensation, incentives, the stock price, or anything else that was even remotely financial in nature. What drove the sense of urgency was a deep concern for what Tabernia was in the process of becoming. What they were most eager for was clear orientation: *What's our plan? What are we to rally behind?* The bottom had dropped out of their market. To be sure, people were nervous about being able to take care of their teams and their families; they wanted to understand how that would all shake out. But what they most deeply wanted was clarity about the mission: *In the marketplace, what is our new problem-to-solve? We don't want a bunch of glib bromides about being the best.*

Part of what fueled the anger in the room was that they had no clue how the comments they'd offered the day before had registered with the leadership team. They were in suspense—they didn't know what to expect. So I paused my teaching and described to them the seriousness with which Nolan and his team had reacted to their input and questions. And I sketched out a change in the day's agenda that would give them the opportunity to tackle all of the issues that troubled them. This took the temperature down to the point where I could finish the material and get out of the room with my shirt still on my back.

In the afternoon, Nolan and his team joined the group. Josh Christopher, Tabernia's head of learning and development, began the session by setting some ground rules. Nolan and his top team would talk for thirty minutes and try to answer the key concerns raised in the previous day's comments. Then there would be a brief break so that the participants, sitting at their tables, could discuss what they'd heard and compile further questions. After that, there would be an open-ended conversation. Finally, at Christopher's suggestion, I would facilitate a conversation *about* the conversation—a meta analysis of what leadership calls for in circumstances as complex, uncertain, and freighted with importance as those Tabernia was now confronting.

Nolan began by putting the problem front and center: "For me, the first *aha!* moment was seeing the looks on your faces the other day when I stood and asked how many of you understood what we were doing here. Not a hand went up. Nobody even nodded. *Big* aha! It reaffirmed a clear calling that something needed to be done."

Having got their attention, Nolan and his team owned up to much of the group's critique while still taking a strong position on the need for change. "We hear that vision matters to you—that it's not a nice-to-have, it's a must-have—and all our talk about our margin rate isn't going to cut it. 'A number isn't a vision.' You want a sense of purpose from us. And you're right—the truth is that we don't have a North Star. But we need one, and you're going to help us get it."

The leadership team went on to discuss what they knew—and didn't know—about the future. They explained the current competitive environment and said emphatically that the business had arrived at a once-in-a-lifetime moment. They told stories that provided context for the realization that things would never be the same. "The company five years from now won't be recognizable."

Where earlier, Nolan and his team had obscured the details and implications of certain proposed changes, they now laid everything out clearly—particularly the realities of shifting resources from established activities to new parts of the business. They admitted to having done too much without careful prioritizing, and having inadvertently caused confusing conflicts between certain groups and activities. They conceded that they were funding things that weren't profitable. And they were forthright in asserting that it just wasn't possible to predict how things would unfold, step by step, over the next few years.

It was an admirable performance. The leaders took risks and made themselves vulnerable without undermining their leadership. If anything, they looked stronger than before. It reminded me of the simple fact that true authority lies in the ability to accept confrontation and dissent. And that, in my opinion, is one of the keys to leading an enterprise through uncertainty, disruption, and ambiguity: people have much more confidence in leaders who are clear-eyed and able to admit that there are limits on what can be reliably known or predicted. Too many leaders haven't gotten that memo.

After wrapping up their initial response to the frank comments from the day before, the leadership team paused before asking the group for its honest reactions. I'd be lying if I said there were no tough questions remaining. But after some spirited back-and-forth, the atmosphere in the room began to calm. What ensued felt like a meaningful conversation, among members of a real community. The group—which had hours earlier behaved as if they couldn't do anything without direction—began to take responsibility for carrying the conversation back to their own people. This should serve as a lesson: Executives, when you do your job, the next level down will do theirs.

Other interesting things began to happen. A little meaning entered the room. Echoing what I heard in my work with the PayPal group, one of the high-potential leaders stood and said quite bravely, "We have to be in the business of solving our clients' problems, not just making money." The comment struck a chord for Nolan. "If you do the right thing for the clients," he said, "if it's really meaningful and relevant, we'll be doing the right thing for the business. I understand that's what we all want, and it should drive every decision we make. I think that maybe that compass was lacking here. We need to have it for every person, so that, when confronted with having to make a decision, you will know the North Star."

This wasn't a perfect or especially neat story. Nolan and his team didn't have everything worked out. The vision was a work in progress. But at least there was a shared understanding of how important it was to complete that work. And that seemed to reassure everyone in the room. And Nolan had not become defensive. Confronted with a particularly tough question, he said, "The thing I love about this is that you care. One thing about having an engaged work force is that you all want to be winners. You want to know the battle plan. You want to be able to define success and be personally committed."

He announced that he wanted to put together a small team, consisting of some of the people in the room, to hammer out a strategy and vision statement. "It's a journey," he said, "to align the thousands of people in this company around a program they really believe in. So we have to get the ball rolling right now."

My impression was that the group was grateful for the response. A number of people thanked Nolan and his team for having been "so open and honest." One person went further, telling Nolan that "honest and true transparency—how you thought about the questions that were raised—actually led to the trust and credibility we were searching for." Another acknowledged the size of the task: "This is hard stuff. Sometimes it hurts to think it through. I am in awe of what we are trying to accomplish. It's significant and real. Lots of futures depend on us getting it right." And someone else said, "I was happy to hear that in five years the company will be unrecognizable. We've never heard that out loud before. If we want to be successful, we really need to be different." The tone, substance, and quality of the comments couldn't have been more different from where the group was two hours earlier. Meaning, motivation, and community had been restored.

As for me, I wiped the sweat from my forehead, threw my hands back behind my head, and lazily watched the group shake hands and say goodbye. It had been a year since, in that plush San Francisco ballroom, my consumer goods client had scripted an elaborate production to present a "new" strategy that turned out to be more sizzle than steak. Ironically, compared to that day, today had been a total mess. And yet it was an honest mess. Instead of smiling for the cameras or reading from a script, Nolan and his team actually listened. They recognized the elephant on the table. They admitted they didn't have the answers. And they promised to find them. It wasn't a storybook ending, but it felt surprisingly good. Nolan and his team had faced up to the responsibility for making big choices on behalf of the business. For at least the time being, they created some clarity.

Epilogue: From Insight to Action

I would not be surprised if many readers recognized certain similarities between their own organizations and one or more of the book's examples. Therefore I want to leave you with some constructive thoughts on how to put those insights to work. Because no matter where you sit on the org chart, there are ways for you to take action.

You are now in a better position to spot the existence of confusion in your own organization, even before it becomes a full-blown crisis. When it comes to addressing the underlying dilemmas that spread confusion, whether you're the CEO or a middle manager, you can expect to encounter strong forces that will push and pull against your desire to act. Some of these forces may be within your organization; some may be within you.

A number of years ago, in a leadership development program for state corrections officers that a friend of mine, Tom Gilmore, was running, an insignificant yet powerful leadership moment took place. During a break between sessions, a somewhat jaded group of wardens began grumbling about a clock on the room's wall that was still unchanged from the start of daylight saving time six weeks earlier.[1] The wardens complained that the clock was yet another—albeit symbolic—example of the state's larger corrections problems: nothing ever changes, broken things fester and multiply, no one takes accountability, and so forth. Then, out of the blue, one of the wardens quietly placed a chair against the wall, climbed up on it, and reset the clock.

When something is broken and stays that way, after a while we tend to stop seeing it. Its brokenness becomes "the new normal." We accept it and factor it into our accommodation of all the other broken things. In the case of a wall clock, we add or subtract the hour each time we look at it. Soon enough, the accommodation itself goes unnoticed, and resignation sets in. What's broken no longer looks quite so wrong. You stop noticing all of the things that are broken. You then fail to connect the dysfunctional consequences back to their true root causes, which—as we have seen in case after case—are often related to the very purpose of the organization.

You might think that the act of fixing the clock was nothing special. But it took courage, in that moment, for the warden to go against his peer group's powerful resignation and skepticism about change. Because of the contrast it created with the sour complaints that had so recently filled the room, the act made a sly point, highlighting the transformative difference between grousing about a problem and actually taking steps to fix it. As a result, there soon came a noticeable shift in the wardens' group dynamic when it came to thinking about how to handle larger problems.

What brings someone from a position of accommodation and going along to the point of taking action? It's more complicated than simply overcoming inertia. You have to find a way to see things differently—to not just see them as needing repair, but see a role for *yourself* in their repair. You yourself have to change. Your thought pattern has to change from "Somebody should fix that clock" to "I really ought to fix that clock." What's needed, then, is a sense of investment and accountability—the recognition that the problem is yours to solve.

On this point, remember Donna Dubinsky at Apple. There was a pivotal moment in which she made the leap from feeling aggrieved and disrespected to feeling empowered enough to act. Dubinsky had just come from her watershed confrontation with CEO John Sculley at an Apple executive retreat. She was worried about her future in the company—all the more so because she had just called out the CEO in a highly charged public way. Back at the office she ran into Del Yocam, head of the Apple II division and someone whom she held in high esteem. Dubinsky sought his advice on the merits of the proposed just-in-time distribution system, which she had so far opposed. Yocam told her plainly that he had no way of evaluating the new strategy—it might or might not work. But he was clear on one thing: if the strategy was the right path for Apple, she should support it; if not, she should put a stop to it. He made it clear that he expected her to figure it out. And he held her accountable for *doing the right thing*.

It took this one pivotal encounter with a senior colleague to activate Dubinsky's inner sense of responsibility and to focus her thinking on what was best for Apple, not for herself. The recognition stiffened her resolve and refocused her thinking. She accepted ownership of the choice and took a stand, thereby putting her Apple career on the line.

On a different level, the need to seize accountability bedeviled Intel founders Andy Grove and Gordon Moore for some time. In retrospect, it seems strange that the two most powerful figures in the company felt so stymied when faced with the choice of abandoning memory chips in favor of microprocessors. Rationally, they knew it was the smart thing to do, but they were torn between internal factions and couldn't muster up the courage to take the final action. Only when they paused to imagine being fired by Intel's board of directors were they able to see that whoever succeeded them would immediately do what they had been dithering about. Recognizing that the good of the company required action gave them permission to do it themselves.

In each of these three examples—the warden, Dubinsky, and Intel's founders—people with different levels of status and power came to accept their responsibility for circumstances that lay within their ability to control. *They embraced their duty to contravene the status quo on behalf of the organization.*

I have come to believe that constructive resistance of this kind can be a profound form of change. These little moments of unsung heroism jostle problems loose. They disclose alternative possibilities for the organization.

Though we often celebrate bold, charismatic leadership, small actions can have disproportionately large effects. The warden who fixed the clock and Dubinsky's ultimatum are examples of what my colleagues Tom Gilmore, Rebecca Blum, and I have elsewhere called "small leadership." By overcoming his feelings of resignation and cynicism, the warden changed the atmosphere in the room simply by climbing onto a chair and resetting the clock. By taking on dysfunctional decision-making processes at Apple, Dubinsky helped put them back into order.

History is full of these moments. Rosa Parks's refusal to give up her seat to a white man on a bus in Montgomery, Alabama, is a classic example of small leadership. Her act of conscience became the defining moment of the civil rights movement. It got the attention of Martin Luther King Jr., who reluctantly allowed the movement to use his church for a protest meeting, warning his friends "Just this one time." Parks's actions led to the Montgomery bus boycott and helped initiate the strategy of nonviolent civil disobedience—the "business model" for social change.[2]

Acts of small leadership can thus have outsized impact. They perform the role of making monumental undertakings more easily achievable. In truth, you don't have to be a top executive to resist, confront, and even reverse the contagious effects of a crisis. If the conflicts in the business can flow down from on high, generating breakdowns throughout the organization, so too can creative solutions and purposeful action flow upward to help resolve the crisis.

Our ability to create disproportionate effects out of small but courageous moments is rooted in remaining attuned to the dynamics unfolding around us, feeling a sense of responsibility to the community, and remaining faithful to the principle of doing the right thing instead of just going along. Within almost every business, at any given moment some person—maybe you are one of them—is incubating an idea (or an action) that swims against the tide of the prevailing enterprise culture and practices. To be sure, many more of those ideas will perish than will flourish. But the ones that thrive make it easier for larger, more fundamental changes to occur. Of all the people at Apple who were plagued by the nagging feeling that something was wrong, it was Dubinsky who took the first hard step of attempting to name it.

It is never easy to go against the tide. In the early days of the PC, the people at IBM who believed in microcomputers faced ardent internal opposition. IBM was then a mainframe-dominated culture, and so-called "micros" were seen as unserious playthings for hobbyist geeks. To insulate themselves from that attitude, the new technology's advocates went south and started a small developmental division in Boca Raton, Florida. That was one small move. Then they—and the fledgling PC industry—got a needed assist from then-unheralded Lotus Development Corporation when it introduced its spreadsheet, Lotus 1-2-3. That new tool turned the PC into a business machine worthy of the IBM brand.

The journey to becoming a change agent begins with the commitment to an idea, whether small or large, and ripens into a felt sense of responsibility: "The clock is wrong, so I need to reset it." "I shouldn't have to give up my seat to that white man." "Personal computers are tools for businesspeople, not toys for geeks." "I don't like what's going on here at Apple, and I have to do something about it."

One person can make a difference.

The Courage to Confront Uncomfortable Facts

Back in 2008, when Twitter was in its infancy, a curious phenomenon took place at the annual South by Southwest (SXSW) music/film/culture/technology event in Austin, Texas. During a general session, a journalist interviewing Facebook founder and CEO Mark Zuckerberg was slow to involve the audience in the Q&A. As the session wore on, audience members started tweeting that the questions were lame and the interview a waste of time. Tweets proliferated and grew more heated. Soon increasingly audible rumblings spread through the seats. Finally someone in the crowd stood up and demanded that the journalist let the audience ask some questions. The journalist seemed affronted, and the petitioner suggested that she check her Twitter feed to see how the session was going over. Twitter had provided those in the hall with a very rare thing: a real-time, glaringly scathing consensus about an unfolding event. As the consensus quickly took shape, the audience felt increasingly empowered to intervene.

Few problems that threaten a business ever go wholly unnoticed. We all know, if only vaguely, when something is broken. But in the main, and unlike the SXSW session, individuals sadly tend to suffer in silence and isolation. We generally don't know, for example, that we have potential allies. We may feel like we're the only ones who see the problem. And, as I mentioned earlier, we unwittingly collude with each other in order to keep the family secret hidden from view. But even when we do realize that something's wrong and that others agree with us, we rarely accept the risks that would come from trying to do something about it. Sadly, it's hard to find a Donna Dubinsky or a Rosa Parks in business.

If you are an executive, this is a big problem. More often than not, leaders don't recognize the spreading discontent until it's too late and you are bushwhacked by a focusing event—such as when, on Black Monday, those fifteen Intel microprocessor scientists walked out the door in frustration. Or when, in late June 2012, CNN got egg on its face when it wrongly reported that the Supreme Court had overturned the individual mandate of the Affordable Care Act. The connection was clear to those in the news organization. "It's outrageous and embarrassing," one staffer told a reporter. "Maybe this will shake the company into understanding that CNN has not been the 'most trusted name in news' for a very long time."[3]

Smart leaders treat such events as a wake-up call not to be wasted. But I would challenge you, if you are a leader, to go one step further. Do not allow things that matter to fester; face up to them early on.

When it's running properly, every business deserves to be called a community. People come together and feel responsible to one another and the guiding purpose of the business. They join in making sure things continue to work as they should. Sustaining purpose over time takes vigilance and work. Even the most carefully chosen purpose will eventually reach its sell-by date and need to be rethought. Over time, customers, markets, competitors, and technology innovations push a business to make compromises. And the compromises inevitably chip away at the business's clarity of purpose. Crises will naturally arise, and new choices will need to be faced. These choices will eventually create contradictions and conflict. But, in business, you have to expect conflict; it simply comes with the territory.

Surprisingly, most leaders resist the inherent conflict in business. Robert McKee, the famous screenwriting and story-telling teacher, once said as much about the dramas that arise in organizational life: "Most companies and executives want to sweep the dirty laundry, the difficulties, the antagonists, and the struggle under the carpet." But those very things, McKee argued, are occasions for heroism—for our rising to, not shrinking from, the defining struggles that make a business great. Like a screenwriter reveling in taut drama, leaders should drag the big, messy problems out into the light.

If we learned anything from Jim Nolan, it was the power that comes from direct confrontation with uncomfortable facts. To be sure, choosing the right purpose demands intelligence, an incisive understanding of the business, and a sure reading of the marketplace. But even more critical is the courage to take responsibility for uncovering the choices that underlie the messy conflicts that plague the business. The leader's primary responsibility is to *take* responsibility.

Remember Longy in this regard. The one-hundred-year-old institution reinvented itself only when Karen Zorn felt compelled to face up to the school's inherent contradictions. Rather than run from the anxieties that animated the crisis, Longy and its leaders moved to tackle them head-on. Their actions vividly illustrate the words of the famous economist John Kenneth Galbraith: "All of the great leaders have had one characteristic in common: it was the willingness to confront unequivocally the major anxiety of their people in their time. This, and not much else, is the essence of leadership."

I want to conclude the book with a clear imperative that holds whether you're an executive or a frontline leader: move toward the anxiety rather than away from it. You know that ubiquitous announcement in train stations and airports around the country: "If you see something, say something"? The same goes in your organization. When you run into evidence of a crisis, don't sit back and get out of the way, don't throw up your hands or shrug your shoulders or roll your eyes. Instead, lean forward. Diagnose. Interpret. Question. Take action.

I urge senior executives, who have the particular responsibility for defining the aims of the larger enterprise, to consider the following:

If the stories in this book have any truth to them, the choices that you may be trying to avoid are the very same choices that can, once they are made, galvanize and ennoble your organization. Confront them. Controversies and tensions, once artfully dodged but now acknowledged and resolved, can generate energy that reinvents your organization. If this seems hard, appreciate that the gains to be had by choosing are great *for exactly the same reason* that Michael Porter has said choice is so frightening. And remember, on this count, that you have the real responsibility. Ultimately the meaning, community, vitality, and above all clarity in your business come from your courage to choose.

Notes

Introduction

1. Theodore Levitt, "Marketing Myopia," *Harvard Business Review*, 38 (July–August 1960): 24–47.
2. Richard Foster, Creative Destruction Whips Through Corporate America, Innosight White Paper, 2012.
3. Y. Q. Mui, "Fading Out of Fashion," *Washington Post*, January 2007, http://www.washingtonpost.com/wp-dyn/content/article/2007/01/09/AR2007010901643.html.
4. K. Benner, "Michael Dell's Dilemma," June 2011. http://tech.fortune.cnn.com/2011/06/13/michael-dells-dilemma/.
5. T. Mullaney, "Drip by Drip, Starbucks Lost What Made It Shine," *Chicago Tribune*, 2013. http://www.chicagotribune.com/chi-starbucks-experience-perspective,0,1699819.story.
6. M. Barbaro, "Wal-Mart's New Strategy Goes Back to Basics: Saving Money." http://www.nytimes.com/2007/03/01/business/worldbusiness/01iht-walmart.4768503.html. March 2007.

Chapter One

1. Todd D. Jick and Mary Gentile, "Donna Dubinsky and Apple Computer, Inc.," HBS Premier Case Collection, February 21, 1986. http://hbr.org/product/donna-dubinsky-and-apple-computer-inc-a/an/486083-HCB-ENG.
2. A. Hertzfeld, "The Times They Are A-Changin'," January 1984. http://www.folklore.org/StoryView.py?story=The_Times_They_Are_A-Changin.txt.

3. K. Smith, "The Movement of Conflict in Organizations: The Joint Dynamics of Splitting and Triangulation." *Administrative Science Quarterly* 47, no. 2 (1989).

4. Ibid.

Chapter Two

1. I am indebted to Elizabeth Hansen for suggesting a method for classifying markets by medium, problems-to-solve, and firms.

2. The story of CNN's struggle over the 8 pm slot was told in J. Zengerle, "Fiddling with the Reception," *New York Times* magazine, August 17, 2003. http://www.nytimes.com/2003/08/17/magazine/17CNN.html.

3. M. Calderone, "CNN Hopes King Ends Evening Slide." *Politico*, January 27, 2010.

Chapter Three

1. M. E. Porter, "What Is Strategy?" *Harvard Business Review*, 1996.

2. S. Stevenson, "The Southwest Secret," June 2012. http://mobile.slate.com /articles/business/operations/2012/06/southwest_airlines_profitability _how_the_company_uses_operations_theory_to_fuel_its_success_.html.

3. C. Zook and J. Allen, *Profit from the Core: A Return to Growth in Turbulent Times* (Boston: Bain & Company, 2010).

4. D. Bennett, "Easy = True," *Boston Globe*, January 2010. http://www .boston.com/bostonglobe/ideas/articles/2010/01/31/easy__true/.

5. E. B. York, "What G Isn't Is a Sales Success," August 2009. http:// adage.com/article/news/gatorade-s-g-campaign-a-sales-success/138368/.

6. Bennett, "Easy = True."

7. E. W. Zuckerman, "The Categorical Imperative: Securities Analysts and the Illegitimacy Discount," *American Journal of Sociology* 104, no. 5 (1999): 1398–1438.

8. E. W. Zuckerman, T. Kim, K. Ukanwa, and J. Von Rittmann, "Robust Identities or Nonentities? Typecasting in the Feature Film Labor Market," *The American Journal of Sociology*, 2003.

Chapter Four

1. H. Drummond, *The Art of Decision Making* (West Sussex, England: Wiley, 2001).

2. M. Cohen, J. March, and J. Olsen, "A Garbage Can Model of Organizational Choice," *Administrative Science Quarterly* 17, no. 1 (March 1972).

3. W. Kiechel III, *The Lords of Strategy: The Secret Intellectual World of the New Corporate World* (Boston: Harvard Business Press, 2010).

4. See M. E. Porter, "What Is Strategy?" *Harvard Business Review*, 1996.

5. Kiechel, *The Lords of Strategy*.

6. Porter, "What Is Strategy?"

7. L. Hirschhorn, "The Primary Risk," *Human Relations*, 52, no. 1 (1999): 5–23.

8. R. Ramanujam and D. M. Rousseau, "Organizational Behavior in Healthcare: The Challenges Are Organizational, Not Just Clinical," *Journal of Organizational Behavior* 27, no. 7 (2006), 809.

9. M. Augier and J. G. March, "Realism and Comprehension in Economics: A Footnote to an Exchange Between Oliver E. Williamson and Herbert A. Simon," *Journal of Economics and Organizational Behavior* 66, no. 1 (2008): 95–105.

Chapter Five

1. R. A. Burgleman, G. W. Cogan, and B. K. Graham, *Strategic Exit and Corporate Transformation: Evolving Links of Technology Strategy and Substantive Generic Corporate Strategies*, Research Paper Series, no. 1406, Graduate School of Business, Stanford University, September 1996.

Chapter Six

1. T. M. Amabile and S. J. Kramer, "Do Happier People Work Harder?" *New York Times*, September 2011. http://www.nytimes.com/2011/09/04/opinion/sunday/do-happier-people-work-harder.html.

2. Personal communication, September 2012.

3. N. Mailer, *The Spooky Art: Some Thoughts on Writing* (New York: Random House, 2003).

4. S. Glucksberg, "The Influence of Strength of Drive on Functional Fixedness and Perceptual Recognition," *Journal of Experimental Psychology* 63, no. 1 (1962): 36–41.

5. C. P. Niemiec, R. M. Ryan, and E. L. Deci, "The Path Taken: Consequences of Attaining Intrinsic and Extrinsic Aspirations," *Journal of Research in Personality* 73 no. 3 (2009): 291–306.

6. P. A. Boyle, A. S. Buchman, L. L. Barnes, and D. A. Bennett, "Effect of a Purpose in Life on Risk of Incident Alzheimer Disease and Mild Cognitive Impairment in Community-Dwelling Older Persons," *Archives of General Psychiatry* 67, no. 3 (2010): 304–310.

7. L. Hirschhorn, "Thinking Together About the Psychodynamics of Strategy," William Alanson White Institute Presentation, April 5, 2010.

8. T. Muller, "Southwest Airlines CEO Kelly on LUV, Leadership and Employee and Customer Satisfaction," October 2009. http://www.today .mccombs.utexas.edu/2009/10/southwest-airlines-ceo-kelly-on-luv -leadership-and-employee-and-customer-satisfaction/.

Epilogue

1. C. Sullivan, R. Blum, and T. Gilmore, "The Power of Small Leadership," *Pfeiffer Annual: Leadership and Development* (2010): 220–232.

2. A. Halsey, "Horton, a Fighter for Rights," *Philadelphia Inquirer*, January 20, 1990, section D, p. 1.

3. K. Fung and J. Mirkinson, "Supreme Court Health Care Ruling: CNN, Fox News Wrong on Individual Mandate" (video), June 2012. http:// www.huffingtonpost.com/2012/06/28/cnn-supreme-court-health-care -individual-mandate_n_1633950.html.

Acknowledgments

Of the myriad organizational dysfunctions I have been hired to help my clients fix over the years, most if not all had to do with leaders avoiding something. Ducking the big issues, I learned, had big consequences—not just for the business, but for everyone involved. Indeed, there are many sad stories I have left out of this book. People can and do get injured by choices not made. There are casualties. Having seen this pattern long enough and witnessed its devastating, yet unrecognized, impact, I took it as my responsibility—one might even say my purpose—to do what I could to help leaders square up to the undiscussable issues that plagued their organizations. This book has been the direct extension of that purpose.

That said, I came to understand something much more profound and more positive about the nature of work as I completed the book. I learned that the greatness of business and its towering achievements arise not from winning in the marketplace, advancing one's career, or garnering all the money and other rewards that success brings. True greatness, I discovered, comes from people coming together in a struggle that imbues the enterprise with meaning, values, and purpose. We spend so much of our lives at work; we are right to expect it to be fulfilling.

This kind of fulfillment arises from the most unlikely situations. The beautiful irony about *The Clarity Principle* is that the very same conflicts and contradictions that subvert performance and often make organizational life feel absurd are at the same time the raw material from which transformation can occur and some measure of greatness can be achieved. Poison and antidote, it turns out, arise from the same source.

It was this paradoxical discovery that led me to have a new faith in business. Business, it turns out, has all the stuff that makes life worth living: significance, struggle, epiphany, enchantment, and the recognition that the best things we do aren't just about us. Hanging out with organizations like Dividio, PayPal, and, yes, even Wall Street banks, showed me that chasing profits and achieving year-over-year growth isn't *really* what business is about—not at its best, anyway. Profits and growth aren't ends in and of themselves. When they are, the achievement tends to be shallow, corrosive, and unsustainable. Material success, when it is rightfully earned, happens when a company lives up to its purpose to solve problems in the world.

This point of view, which one might call a *humanistic* view of business, found its voice for me in this book. I am grateful for that discovery. But looking back over the journey here tells me that the roots of this particular stance go further back to a number of important people and institutions who deserve recognition. Without them I would never have been able to write this book.

The first early iteration of *The Clarity Principle* was a paper I wrote with Lynn Langdon, a client of mine and the chief operating officer of the American Board of Internal Medicine (ABIM). For those who have never heard of the organization, the ABIM is a venerable medical institution whose job it is to establish physician standards of practice. Setting standards is a big leadership job, and the ABIM does it remarkably well. They're also one of the most thoughtful organizations around. I owe them a great deal. Not only did I cut my consulting teeth doing strategy work for the ABIM, but they were willingly to let me air their dirty laundry for the sake of learning.

Back in 2008, Lynn and I presented the nascent ideas that would later become this book at a symposium hosted by the International Society for the Psychoanalytic Study of Organizations (ISPSO). The mission of ISPSO is to use psychoanalysis to better understand organizational life. It is a quirky, maddening, but ultimately lovable institution. And like the ABIM, ISPSO was a place that gave me the space and encouragement to try out new ideas. For that I am very grateful, especially to former President Jim Krantz.

While the ABIM and ISPSO were giving me room to try out new things, much of the intellectual stimulus for the book came from my colleagues at the Center For Applied Research (CFAR). CFAR had been an experimental fusion of disciplines like strategy, operations, and economics with the social sciences including psychology and anthropology. I called CFAR home for almost eight years, though it felt like a whole lot longer. I met my wife, Elizabeth, there, as well as most of my mentors and many, many friends.

Three CFAR colleagues made an indelible imprint on me and this book, and they deserve recognition. The first was Larry Hirschhorn. This book is in large part a continuation of Larry's substantive work on the psychology of strategy. Larry is one of the most penetrating thinkers I have ever met, and beyond that, a wise compassionate man. I am grateful to have closely worked with him. If ever there was one, I am a proud Hirschhornian.

At any office, it's all about where you sit. At CFAR I had the pleasure of having an office directly across from two people who had a huge influence on my work. One of these was Tom Gilmore. Tom has a wonderful habit of stringing together cultural and literary references, historical anecdotes, allusions, and obscure quotes from outside the world of business to enliven a point. Who needs Lou Gerstner when you have Odysseus? Tom's anecdotes must have had an effect on me, because halfway through the book I found myself adopting his penchant for making such connections. But beyond inheriting his unique style, I have depended over the years on Tom's kindness, encouragement, and care. He has been a true mentor.

Nancy Drozdow sat next to Tom, and together we formed a little triangle in the corner office in downtown Philadelphia. The distance between my office and Nancy's was too far to carry on a conversation at normal levels but short enough that we could successfully yell back and forth, which we did frequently, and to the annoyance of our colleagues. It was Nancy who taught me strategy in the first place. But she also taught me values. Whatever moral grounding moors this book in place, it comes from my time working with Nancy. No one does strategy with more heart and guts than she does.

The book had been in gestation for five long years, but I delivered it in nine grueling months. There were a lot of people who helped make that happen. Even before the writing began, my editor at Jossey-Bass, Genoveva Llosa, was right there at the most important moments. The book was something very different before Genoveva came onto the scene. She encouraged me to change directions and follow my passion. I owe her big thanks for that.

Lew McCreary deserves a special acknowledgment. There wasn't a person on the planet more perfectly suited to help me with the writing than Lew. He was the ideal mentor and companion. I was truly blessed to have had him by my side.

In 2011 I left CFAR to join an up-and-coming start-up firm called Pivot. *The Clarity Principle* would not have come into existence had I not been so encouraged and inspired by my Pivot colleagues. I am especially grateful to David Dotlich for having placed his faith in this book and for the support of my long-time friend and colleague Stacey Philpot. David and Stacey believed in this project like nobody else. I was also fortunate to have a lot of other Pivot help along the way, especially from Ron Meeks, Cade Cowan, my dear Julie Aiken, Michaelene Kyrala, Alex Libson, Rebecca Blum, Angela Flocco, and Christine Linder.

None of the book would have happened without my amazing clients, both those identified and those whose identities I masked in this book. Their willingness to learn, reflect, and entertain new possibilities inspired me and gave me a reason to do my work. Special thanks go to Rob Killion and the board of directors at the Common Application, Karen Zorn at the Longy School, and Dianne Mills at PayPal for allowing me to use their stories.

Finally, there aren't enough pages to fully acknowledge the role that my wife, Elizabeth, played in helping make this book possible. The first glimmers of *The Clarity Principle* go back almost six years ago to the birth of our daughter Sophia. Since then, we have had two more children, Abraham and Lyra; moved three times; changed jobs; and overcome many, many obstacles. When I wrote the book in 2012 it was one of the hardest years in my life. Elizabeth sacrificed so that I could write, and she endured my obsessive behavior over the last year. But beyond her loving support while I wrote the book, I owe Elizabeth a major intellectual debt. I have depended on the subtlety of her thinking and intuitive feeling for the material in this book more times than I can count. Indeed, some of best insights in these pages came from our conversations. Elizabeth, I want to thank you from the bottom of my heart.

About the Author

Chatham Sullivan is an organizational psychologist and a partner at Pivot, a strategic leadership boutique. Chatham has taught at the Wharton School of Business and the School of Social Policy at the University of Pennsylvania and worked closely with executives at some of the worlds most influential organizations, such as PayPal, eBay, Nike, Johnson & Johnson, and other Fortune 500 companies. Chatham is an avid fly fisherman and once worked as a professional guide on Wyoming's Platte River. He currently lives in Belmont, Massachusetts, with his wife, Elizabeth, and their three children, Sophia, Abraham, and Lyra.

For more information, please visit www.pivotleadership .com.

Index